p. 138

Barriers Between Women

Barriers Between Women

Paula J. Caplan, Ph.D
Psychologist
Family Court Clinic
Clarke Institute of Psychiatry
and
Assistant Professor
Department of Psychiatry
University of Toronto
Toronto, Canada

SP MEDICAL & SCIENTIFIC BOOKS

New York

SPECTRUM PUBLICATIONS, INC.
175-20 Wexford Terrace, Jamaica, N.Y. 11432

Library of Congress Cataloging in Publication Data

Caplan, Paul J
    Barriers between women.

    Includes index.
    1. Women—Psychology. 2. Mother and daughter.
3. Hostility (Psychology) I. Title.
HQ1206.C26   155.3′2   80-12983
ISBN 0-89335-103-2

This book is dedicated
to
my parents
Theda Ann Karchmer Caplan
and
Jerome Arnold Caplan
and
my children
Jeremy Benjamin
and
Emily Julia

Contents

Preface

This book is an exploration of some of the psychological and so-cial-psychological factors that have created barriers between women. Particular attention is paid to the daughter-mother relationship.

The content is based on psychotherapy material, test results and conversations with patients and non-patients across a wide age span. I acquired the material in my various roles as a clinician, researcher and theorist—and, always, as a woman, with whatever special biases and special understandings that might involve.

Because much of the book deals with the development of wom-en's difficulties in relationships with other women, the emphasis will often be on how the growing daughter feels in her relationship with her mother. The mother's feelings will be discussed very little for two reasons: to limit the scope of this book and because much of what applies to the daughter also applies to the mother. It is often due to her own experiences as a daughter that the mother encounters difficulty in rearing her own daughter or feeling com-fortable about her ability to do so. But it is important for the reader to keep in mind throughout the book that child-rearing is a frighten-ing, difficult task at least part of the time for virtually every mother. In any long-term relationship, one begins to experience one's own needs, and it is simply human to wish that the other person in the relationship (even an infant or young child) would meet those needs. What matters to the child's healthy develop-ment, however, is both the intensity of the wish and the extent to which the mother arranges to meet her own needs from other sources. The main point of this is to draw the reader's attention to the fact that, though I will be describing mainly the daughter's feelings, it is clearly a complex and difficult relationship for the mother as well.

Much of the book is an exploration of sources of conflict, with a view toward prevention, but it is not the case that conflict is always undesirable and does not facilitate growth. Understanding its nature and sources is essential, so that we can try to prevent it when it threatens to become pathological or growth-limiting.

I do not believe that any of my observations apply to all women and girls. I intend the content of the book to comprise suggestions that can promote discussion, association, questioning and further exploration. Very little is understood about women's relationships with other women. Many important aspects, such as the daughter-mother relationship and lesbianism, are more difficult to scrutinize without allowing the most primitive kinds of fears to blur our vision, and it would be naive to claim certainty for any of my suggestions; however, I have described only those trends for which I have found substantial empirical and/or clinical support.

I presented some of the ideas for this book to a group of women who were in their late twenties and thirties, and who were mothers of toddlers. They all were daughters, of course, and many had daughters of their own. Kathryn Morgan, a joint professor of philosophy and women's studies, observed this discussion and pointed out that their comments about problems in the daughter-mother relationship followed a consistent pattern. Nearly all the women who spoke denied that their relationships with their mothers were problematic. They expressed love, gratitude and admiration for their mothers, even when a more or less patronizing quality intruded ("For her era, she was really very liberated"). But when it came to discussing the problems they encountered in raising their own daughters, nearly all had strong feelings—of fear, awe, hope —about their conflicts and problems. These were the very conflicts and problems that they denied having had with their own mothers.

It is possible but unlikely that so many women had nearly perfect mothers and yet felt they had many difficulties to overcome in raising their own daughters. What seemed more likely, and what has since become clearer to me, was that these women were simply acting in their accustomed role of defending their mothers against the possible criticisms of society. The notion that motherhood is sacred had to be protected, and they were reluctant to point fingers of blame. This made it difficult for them to honestly examine their own feelings.

When writing about phenomena such as those presented in this book, one cannot be sure how much one's own wishes, needs and disappointments have shaped the conclusions. But at this stage in the social changes that are affecting all of women's relationships, and at this stage in the growth of psychology of women, to draw attention to some issues and problems is the logical step.

Acknowledgements

The ideas for this book were born in Ronald deSousa's course in philosophy and psychoanalysis, sparked by his careful and exciting style of thinking and teaching. Kathryn Morgan's combination of emotional and intellectual involvement in the feminist movement and personal feminism was inspiring; Kathryn also arranged for and encouraged early public presentations of this work, the first of which was to the Canadian Society of Women in Philosophy. I am grateful to that group, and Barbara Houston in particular, for their comments.

Ethel Strainchamps and Carolyn Watson provided early encouragement, and Bruce Caplan, Alan Rauzin and Corinne Wilks read and made helpful suggestions on an early draft. Frances Newman and Fred Weinstein did likewise on a portion of a later draft.

Fraser Clark urged me to get on with it, and he and William Karchmer provided rooms of my own in which to do the writing.

Georgina White kept up my spirits and made many useful, pertinent suggestions during every phase of the last stages of preparation.

The loving care that Maria Matias and Christina Schaelin showed both my children and me provided time and relaxation for doing this work.

Susan Naborczyk patiently did the lion's share of the typing of the manuscript, making warm, supportive comments all the way. Additional help with typing and proofreading came from Elisabeth Bramberger, Elaine Gulliver, Joan Hutton, Janet Sedgwick, Ellen Spiegel, Betty St. Jean and Helen Trahan.

To my grandmother Gertrude Gorbach Caplan and to the memory of my grandmother Esther Milner Karchmer, from whom I learned much about women's lives, I owe what goes beyond words.

Introduction

One of the most complex psychological questions raised by the New Feminism is that of women's relationships with other women. The feminism of the sixties and seventies is distinguished from earlier such movements by an emphasis on "consciousness-raising" groups in which women often talk about the emotional barriers that interfere with their working together in open, productive, noncompetitive ways, free from jealousy and anger.

Many successful career women preface statements with the words "Now, I'm not a Women's Libber but . . ." and finish by saying something like "I believe in equal pay for work of equal value," which is a feminist principle. Kome wrote in *Homemaker's* magazine (1977): "Women seem to be espousing feminist principles, on the one hand, and dissociating themselves from the movement on the other. . . . Letters in response to our articles are touching, personal and supportive. Many readers are eager to report discrimination, or to recount how they handled being treated in a patronizing manner, or succeeded despite obstacles. Yet, when I introduce myself as a feminist, many women react as though the term were scatological. . . ." (p. 72B) Why do these women want so much to be considered separate from other women? Indeed, when asked, they often go so far as to say they do not believe in affirmative action programs by public and private groups to help more women in self and career development. "*I* didn't need any help like that" is a typical answer. They seem to lack a sense of solidarity.

Somehow, we are not surprised to find successful women setting themselves apart and feminists having to work hard to lower the barriers. After all, the prevalent stereotype of women in our society is that they cannot work together, even though problems in this area arise between males as well. If we wish to increase women's potential for working with and helping each other, it is essential that we understand how the stereotype developed and the extent to which it may be accurate. Only then can we begin to overcome the barriers.

Since the time of Freud, who suggested that how people interact with women is heavily influenced by their childhood experiences with their mothers, little has been written from the standpoint of individual and interpersonal psychology about women's conflicts with other women. Still less of value has been written about the prototype of female-female interactions, the mother-daughter relationship. For the most part, only the novelists have ventured to describe the unpleasant aspects of the mother-daughter relationship; they are protected by the ongoing literary-critical debate over how much of a writer's "fiction" must have come from direct experience. Those of the nonfiction writers who have discussed the relationship have tended to idealize it, to use the form of advice-column prescriptions and "how-to" recipes, to take moralizing tones or to base their analyses on largely one-dimensional theories that unquestioningly accept Freudian doctrine and the effects of sexist socialization. Beyond sex and death, the relationship between mother and daughter has been protected from inquiry and investigation by everyone's fear of what we might find. Society has traditionally wanted daughters to grow to be mothers. To suggest that a daughter might have been dissatisfied with her mother, might have had an unsatisfactory role model for good mothering, is disconcerting. In particular, to find a female expressing feelings other than warmth, acceptance and satisfaction with her lot is distressing because it does not fit the female stereotype.

As contemporary historians and psychologists identify the gaps in knowledge in their respective fields, it is becoming clear that issues that have been important in the lives of men have received higher priority in the eyes of scholars choosing where to apply their energies than issues of importance to women. History has been more a description of men's activities than of women's or even families'. Psychological theories have also been more concerned with issues of importance to males than to females. Since many of the sources of barriers between women are rooted in women's second-class role, the stability of society as we know it may be threatened by an understanding of this status.

For these reasons, combined with the natural fear of examining anything important and traditional, the study of mothers' relationships with their daughters has been impressively neglected. In *Of Woman Born,* perhaps the most honest and detailed exploration of motherhood yet written, Rich (1976) says: "We acknowledge Lear (father-daughter split), Hamlet (son and mother), and Oedipus (son and mother) as great embodiments of the human tragedy; but there is no presently enduring recognition of mother-daughter passion and rapture." (p. 237)

This book is an attempt to consider the sources of barriers between women, with special emphasis on traditional expectations of society that have helped create these barriers and on the daughter-mother relationship in particular.

The single fact with which we begin in trying to understand the conflict between daughters and mothers is that society classifies them both as female. While still very young, the daughter has the capacity *to recognize her similarity* with her mother, both physically and as they are viewed by a society concerned with rules of behavior that depend on one's sex. In this capacity lie the seeds for feelings of both alliance and hostility between them. Without this basic identity, the nature of the daughter-mother relationship would be very different. In societies like ours, many of the answers to the daughter's questions "What may I do?" and "How am I supposed to feel?" begin with the words "Since you are a girl . . ."

One question to keep in mind throughout this book is whether daughter-mother hostility and conflict are universal, with the implication that it may be unavoidable or perhaps even necessary. The question might be answered with extensive anthropological data, combined with reliable information about the unconscious as well as evident feelings that daughters have for their mothers, from cultures all over the world. But there is another way to approach the topic: by considering the nature and function of hostility.

Hostility can be usefully contrasted with both indifference and love. If I feel love for certain people, I am likely to want to move toward them; if I feel indifference, I am likely to allow them to remain wherever they are and want to take no particular action with respect to them; if I feel hostility, I am likely to want to take some action in order to hurt them or drive them away. Love involves a disposition to move toward; hostility involves a disposition to move against. Yet both love and hostility involve wishes to control or direct the activity of the people for whom we have those feelings.

Love clearly serves the evolutionary function of increasing the cohesiveness of pairs of people: e.g., heterosexual couples, for purposes of reproduction; parent-child pairs, for purposes of protection and nurturance of the young. What evolutionary function might hostile feelings serve? Within close relationships, they facilitate the development of independence of the young from the parent generation of the species. A parent who becomes tired of taking care of the young may begin to feel an increased wish for privacy, freedom or a change in activity, and a young child who limits the fulfillment of those wishes may become the object of that parent's hostility. Because hostility tends to be accompanied by a wish to hurt or to send away, it will be to the advantage of such a child to become more independent.

In addition, a child whose innate disposition is to progress through developmental stages from dependency toward greater capacities for independence, self-protection and self-determination will be likely to develop hostility toward obstacles to that goal. Sometimes the obstacles may be inanimate: "Oh, I hate being fifteen. I can't wait till I'm sixteen." But more often the obstacles are people (or are regarded as such by the child). Parents' setting of restrictions are causes of children's hostility. To children, the very presence of parents, whom they regard as having enormous scope for freedom of activity and self-direction, may be a cause of intense hostility when that freedom interferes with their own.

The independence of its members is a crucial element in the survival of a species. From this standpoint, hostility would seem to be a necessary part of the development of individuals into adulthood. Cultural differences would then be expected to be enormous and to depend on a number of factors. These would include:

(1) To what extent is the development of a child overseen by a single individual or a few individuals? The more this task is spread among large numbers of people, the less we would expect to find a child continuing to direct intense hostility toward only one or two adults.

(2) To what extent does a culture have clear guidelines for the times when steps toward independence are encouraged or allowed in the developing youngsters? The greater the ambiguity, the more confusion the youngster will experience, and the more likely it will be that the youngster feels angry about the difficulties of becoming independent without clear permission or instruction.

(3) To what extent do the caretakers of the young feel unambi-

valently pleased when the young become independent? If those charged with the task of encouraging independence end up feeling useless, alone and frightened when their young have achieved independence, such emotions will have an effect similar to that of unclear cultural prescriptions: they will make the process of becoming independent confusing to the young person, who will sense that the caretaker is giving impossible instructions, a double message— "I am telling you to become independent (because society instructs me to tell you that), and I don't want you to become independent (because I will be left alone, frightened, and useless if you do)."

(4) How real is the independence toward which the caretakers are urging the young? In the case of most young girls in North America, for example, the urging is toward the independence to run a household and raise children, but this is usually inseparable from intense dependency on another (the husband who provides financial support, social status and, often, the primary contact with the world outside the home). The more young people feel urged toward supposed independence that really involves dependence, the more hostility are they likely to feel toward the caretaker who is deepening and narrowing their channel for this development. This is intensified still further if, as discussed in (3), the caretaker is ambivalent about the young person becoming independent, since this means the caretaker is dissatisfied with his or her own role but is training the child to fit into that very role. It would be less than human to love unambivalently people who tried to help one fit into the same unhappy mold in which they are living.

We do not know whether daughter-mother hostility is universal and inevitable. But, considering the issues listed above, we can begin to think about such questions as: When hostility is present, what factors have aggravated or mitigated its intensity? Whether or not it is universal, what can be done to change the prevalence of hostility or its destructive manifestations? How can we help daughters to have fuller relationships with their mothers and to have less difficult relationships with other women? How can mothers strengthen their daughters, and how can women strengthen other women?

Any relationship between two people is affected by at least the following: the experiences of each, the way they interpret their experiences, their political attitudes, the society in which they live, and the history of that society. Therefore, although this book is primarily psychological in orientation, references to other fields of study will be mentioned when relevant. The common pathway that all of these factors follow is through the thoughts of the daughter and the mother. Elements of history, politics and culture affect a relationship because of the way they are experienced and interpreted by the people who form the relationship. Those now in the process of being created and transmitted to the next generation can be changed. So, too, can the ways the next generation interprets what happens to them. Our daughters can be helped either more or less to understand what happens. They can be encouraged to allow the continuation of the destructive aspects of hostility toward their mothers and other women, so that society can be preserved in its present state, or they can be encouraged to believe that their actions can help to transform the destructiveness into warmth and mutual support. The latter both requires and will cause changes in things as they are.

CHAPTER 1

General Theory

Two kinds of theories can provide some useful background for understanding why the daughter's awareness of her similarity to her mother profoundly affects their relationship. One, derived from social psychology, concerns the way the daughter-mother pair belongs to, overlaps and is excluded from various groups. The other, from developmental psychology, concerns the daughter's identification with her mother. The parts of these theories that are relevant to this book are presented in the following sections.

In-groups and Out-groups

By the time she is two or three years old, the daughter recognizes that, at least in some ways, she belongs to the same "group," or gender, as her mother. While this might result in a pleasant feeling, the daughter may also resent the tie if membership of the same sex makes it hard for her to differentiate herself from her mother (or to persuade other people to treat her differently from the way they treat her mother). It is helpful to understand how people are affected by believing they belong to certain groups. Social scientists use the word "in-group" to denote a group to which one belongs; "out-groups" are groups from which one is excluded.

The following is a summary of some characteristics of conflict within and between such groups as discussed by Coser (1956, pp. 71–118).

When conflict occurs within a close group, the hostility of one side toward the other increases the more the conflict is felt to be a threat to the group's unity and identity (Coser, 1956). The mother-daughter pair constitutes a very close "group," both members of which are female. The pair exists in a society whose rules have severely limited the lives of its females when compared to its males. If mother or daughter feels it is important to keep within society's constraints, her membership in this pair may represent a refuge: at least here she is free from the unevenness in economic and political power that is present in most male-female pairs. (This is not to say that differences do not exist between a daughter's and a mother's power, but rather that they are not due to the mostly immutable facts of physical differences). In an important sense, the feeling of shelter that daughter and mother may experience within their relationship often arises from their tacit agreement *not* to challenge society's restrictions on females. Once the conflict between their pair and the male world "out there" is minimized, the two can proceed to enjoy their own relationship as much as possible and to seek fulfillment there. Naturally, then, if the daughter and/or mother decides to break social "rules," this poses a threat to their relationship. First, it means that some of their energy is now directed outside the pair. Second, if only one of them breaks the rules, this constitutes an implicit critism, or at least questioning, of the other's obedience to them.

Within a group, conflict can be a means of achieving unity. This is more likely to occur if the conflict concerns goals, values or interests that do not contradict the basic assumptions upon which the relationship is founded (Coser, 1956). As long as a mother and daughter argue about superficial issues or matters that do not question the value or structure of their relationship, the conflict can help strengthen that relationship. (I use the word "strengthen" not necessarily to signify an improvement in a moral sense but only to mean an increase in the chances that their relationship will continue and that they will not feel it is threatened.) Some angry or aggressive feelings inevitably arise in close relationships, and these feelings must be dealt with in some way. If the daughter says, "I wish you weren't my mother," or vice versa, the relationship is threatened. But if mother and daughter can argue furiously about what color the new drapes in the daughter's room should be, the anger will have found at least a partially satisfactory outlet and will be less likely to burst out unexpectedly in ways that threaten the relationship with disintegration. Furthermore, an outlet such as the argument about the drapes is a kind of affirmation of the relationship. Society considers it appropriate for mothers and daughters to make decisions about drapes, so the argument is a way to carry out the rules: "We are really a mother and a daughter, because here we are, arguing about drapes!"

Conflict between one's in-group and an out-group increases internal cohesion (when there is an outside threat thought to be a menace to the group as a whole) (Coser, 1956). Anger felt by daughters toward their mothers has long been thought to increase in early adolescence. Before that time, there tends to be much discussion of a conspiratorial sort between the two about males: "We won't tell your father how much we spent on this dress," or "Mommy, how can I get Bob to like me?" Males are regarded as an out-group, and this draws mother and daughter closer in their attempts to attract, manipulate or defend themselves against those males. But the developing young girl's interest in a male her own age usually reaches a point where the mother becomes part of an out-group, while daughter and boyfriend form an in-group. At this stage, further conflict with her mother tends to increase the daughter's alliance with her boyfriend; in fact, the daughter may consciously or unconsciously arrange to argue with her mother as a way to move closer to her boyfriend, or to resolve a feeling that she has to choose between him and her family.

Conflict between groups, if constant, tends to cause intolerance of dissent within those groups. The only way to solve the problem of internal dissent is through the dissenter's voluntary or forced withdrawal. A group engaged in constant battle with another group needs all its energy for the struggle; it cannot allow conflict within the group to usurp energy or time (Coser, 1956). All mothers in our society have been subject to society's expectations for mothers, whether or not they have wanted to meet them. After becoming a mother, a woman knows she is expected to behave in certain ways. The tendency is strong to seek support and sympathy from individuals who are both similar and available nearby. Daughters meet both these requirements. In particular, mothers who have few other close relationships with females are likely to feel frightened and lonely when conflict with their daughters threatens to deprive them of this source of support in the struggle either to meet, or to fight against, the constant demands society places on them.

Rigidly organized groups may actually search for enemies with the deliberate purpose or unwitting result of maintaining unity and internal cohesion (against real or imagined threats). The evolution of an outer enemy or the invention of such an enemy strengthens social cohesion against threats from within. Similarly, search for or invention of a dissenter within may serve to maintain a structure that is threatened from outside (Coser, 1956). Mothers who are afraid their daughters will leave them alone, either physically or emotionally, often feel a need to prevent their leaving. In this case, feeling that men have most of the power in a society that oppresses women, they may behave as though all males, particularly those within or close to the family, aid and abet that oppression. In some cases, their actions may be justified by the men's behavior; in others, their actions may be disproportionate to the men's energy in supporting the system, or they may be totally unjustified. In all three cases, however, if mother and daughter regard the men as inimical to them, their own relationship is thereby consolidated.

Conflicts in which the participants feel they are merely the representatives of a group, fighting not for self but only for group ideals, are likely to be more radical and merciless than those fought for personal reasons (Coser, 1956). This accurately describes the behavior of many mothers who dutifully carry out society's instructions for them: they teach their daughters to be "ladylike," unassertive, self-denying and nurturant. Such women may have spent unhappy and unfulfilled years because they felt restricted to those kinds of behavior; nevertheless, as society's channel for transmitting its values to its young, they continue teaching their daughters how to live that same kind of life. It is small wonder that these women are often the most shrill and rigid defenders of the status quo that makes women unhappy; they cannot defend the status quo from a basis of a self-confident, active life, and so they defend it as representatives of "the role," a lonely, hollow activity. The activity and aggression that their role prevents them from using constructively produce the stridency with which they defend and perpetuate the causes of their own, and potentially their daughters', despair.

The Cognitive-Developmental Theory of Identification

The "cognitive-developmental" approach to personality theory, delineated by Kohlberg and Zigler (1967), is helpful in exploring the daughter-mother relationship.

Kohlberg and Zigler discuss the process of identification, in which a child takes an individual (usually an adult) as a role model and then attempts to behave like the model. Ultimately, the child adopts not only the overt behavior but also the standards and feelings of the model, at least as the child perceives them. According to the theory, a daughter's process of identification begins with her recognition that she belongs to the same category as her same-sex parent. Thus the theory is based on the postulate that identification depends largely on cognitive growth: The daughter perceives physical similarities between herself and her mother, and physical differences between herself and her father. Because her thinking is concrete at this stage, she is likely to assume that these striking physical characteristics classify her in some important way. She learns that she is "a girl, like Mommy," and she accepts this as a fact. Knowing who she is, how others regard her, and to what groups (e.g., gender-group) she belongs provides her with a sense of certainty and security: "I am a girl, and girls behave in this way, dress this way, feel this way. I know, because I see my mommy do that. So now I know what I am supposed to do."

According to Kohlberg and Zigler, people have a tendency to place positive value on acts and things they believe to be consistent with their conceived identity. Thus in identification the daughter finds a way to fulfill what she believes herself to be: she is female—that is her identity—and the more of her mother's attributes she can take on, the better she feels. She notices that she is doing more and more female things. It seems reasonable to us that the rewards come both from other people, since society positively reinforces those who fit into their sex stereotypes, and from an inner sense, perhaps a sense of competence (White, 1959) at being female and doing a good job of it. Kohlberg and Zigler, however, place little importance on the social reinforcement notion. Because the child knows she is female, they say, praise from her mother and praise for acting girl-like are more reinforcing than praise from males and other kinds of praise. In other words, Kohlberg and Zigler suggest that the value of the praise itself arises as *a result of* the child's classifying herself according to sex. Consistent with their emphasis on the importance of cognition, they propose that the stability of the child's sex-role identity and her ability to use it in the process of identification depends on her ability to conserve and to perceive object constancy. In other words, the clearer she becomes about concepts like "we females," the more she understands what it means to be one of those females, what things females do, and so on.

In Kohlberg and Zigler's theory, the child's primary concern is a kind of self-actualization: If I am female, my great desire is to do as many female things as possible. How do I decide what is female? Well, my mother is female, so I'll do what she does. Identification, then, according to this theory, is a process of clarifying and living out one's identity. What is crucial for Kohlberg and Zigler is the hypothesis that an intimate part of the identification process is the child's need to feel a sense of competence, security and certainty, and freedom from anxiety. These are some of the sources of pleasure experienced by the child while maximizing the similarities between herself and her mother. As we shall see, they also constitute some of the most serious sources of daughter-mother hostility. The daughter discovers that becoming more and more like her mother brings her up against the restrictions of the female role in our society. Nevertheless, the daughter will find it difficult to stop the process of increasing her similarity to her mother, because this would mean giving up the pleasures and rewards inherent in the process. The pleasures she would have to forgo are powerful, since each new achievement of similarity to her mother is part of a fabric that evokes all the pleasures that her prior achievements of similarity produced. In this way, her relationship with her mother lands her in a conflict: she is torn between accepting unpleasant restrictions on her behavior in order to become "female" and sacrificing the pleasures attendant upon becoming "female."

CHAPTER 2

Women's Relationships with Women

Freud's Theory of Daughters and Mothers

The relationships between daughters and mothers have been explored most thoughtfully by Sigmund Freud, and his work heavily influenced the most recent examinations of the subject (Hammer, 1976; Friday, 1977). What Freud wrote about girls and women has undergone intense criticism, and I shall suggest some reservations about his theory. First, however, I shall discuss what he considered to be two major sources of daughters' hostile feelings toward their mothers. It is important to present Freud's theory here both because of its effect on modern thinking about daughters and because it exemplifies the depth and extent of articulation that thought about these matters deserves.

Stated briefly, Freud said that two major sources of daughters' hostility toward their mothers are "penis envy" and daughters' "insatiable," immoderate demands for love and nurturance.

Penis Envy

Freud (1957, 1961b) assumed that all children wish to have a penis. The boy is lucky because he has one, but he is faced with the major worry of guarding his precious organ against damage and loss ("castration anxiety").

The girl feels unlucky, Freud suggests, because she has no penis, and she attributes her bad fortune to fantasied castration: she believes that she, as well as all women, once had a penis but was castrated. According to Freud (1964), several things follow from this. One is that the little girl harbors the wish for a penis ("penis envy"). Freud (1961b) writes of the girl: "To an incredibly late age

7

she clings to the hope of getting a penis some time. That hope becomes her life's aim. . . ." (p. 229) Furthermore, she wishes to give birth to a child as a kind of replacement for her "missing" organ. Accordingly, one reason women desire a sexual relationship with a man is that that temporarily provides them with a penis and can lead to bearing a child, a penis replacement (or "penis-baby").

Another consequence of the girl's lack of a penis, Freud says, is her feeling that she is generally inferior. The girl extends this feeling to a belief that all females are inferior, and since the group of "all females" includes her mother, she grows to regard her with contempt as well. This feeling about her mother is based on self-hatred: I hate my mother because she is just like me in this deficient way. In addition, since children believe their parents are all-powerful, the girl thinks: My mother gave birth to me and takes care of me; she could have given me a penis, but did not; she is to blame. As Freud (1932) wrote, "Girls hold their mother responsible for their lack of a penis and do not forgive her for being thus put at a disadvantage." (p. 124) Hence there arises another source of daughter-mother hostility.

The "Insatiable" Need for Love and Nurturance

In his essay "Femininity" (1964), Freud says that "the child's avidity for its earliest nourishment is altogether insatiable" (p. 122) and that children's "demands for love are immoderate, they make exclusive claims and tolerate no sharing." (p. 123) Though he uses the word "child," and not "daughter" or "girl-child," and while he does not deny that they apply to male children as well, he offers these descriptions of children's needs in the context of explaining why daughters develop hostile feelings toward their mothers. When he wrote about sons' hostility toward their fathers, he attributed that feeling to fear of castration by the father and resentment of the father's greater power and achievements. In discussing daughters and mothers, he cites (1961b) the daughter's fear of losing her mother's love and the daughter's anger at the restrictions her mother places on her behavior, and in that context he emphasizes the notion of the child's unmeetable needs for affection and nurturance.

Freud (1964) describes the daughter's anger at the birth of each new sibling, who takes part of her mother's attention (and, she fears, affection) away from her. He suggests that the daughter is also angry because her mother can never satisfy her sexual needs. Again, writing of grown women but not describing grown men in that way, he says that for women "to be loved is a stronger need for them than to love." (p. 132).

In the same essay, Freud proposes that anthropological data may justify the daughter's feeling that she is inadequately nurtured by her mother. He points out that even mothers who choose to breast-feed their infants in Western cultures usually wean them after a few months, whereas in other cultures children are allowed to nurse for as long as several years.

Considering the intensity of the infant daughter's love for her mother, Freud (1961b) asserts that this positive feeling is probably inevitably paired with angry feelings of equal intensity. Again he invokes a comparison with so-called "primitive" societies, in which, he says, one also finds this pairing of intensely felt opposites. We would suggest that, if this theory is correct, this dualism is probably related to the daughter's extreme dependence on the mother. When the mother meets her needs, the daughter feels intensely grateful and protected, but when her needs are unmet she feels extremely angry at the mother, whom she has identified as the person who is supposed to meet these needs. The very closeness of the early relationship, then, would give rise to hostility between daughter and mother.

In brief summary, Freud attributed daughters' hostility toward their mothers to the daughter's placing blame on the mother for failing to give her a penis and to meet her "insatiable" needs.

Identification

Another aspect of Freudian theory should be noted here which, unlike the two sources of daughter-mother hostility discussed above, applies to both daughters and sons. Freud suggested that children of both sexes come to resent their same-sex parents at the "Oedipal" stage in early childhood, when they wish to win the affections of their opposite-sex parents. The child desires the opposite-sex parent and the same-sex parent intervenes, making the child aware of both the impossibility and moral reprehensibility of that desire. At the same time, the child fears that its desire for the same-sex parent will anger the other parent. Freud believed that children deal with their combined love and fear of the same-sex parent by putting to use their knowledge that they and the same-sex parent belong to the same gender group. They try to become like the same-sex parent in order to avoid that parent's anger; at the same time, they hope to become enough like the same-sex parent to attract a person of the other sex.

Both girls and boys begin with the mother as their original, primary love object, the person who meets their needs and to whom they are closest emotionally. Later, the daughter regards her mother as an obstacle to fulfilling her desire for her father and thus resents her primary love object, who has become an obstacle in the path to her second object. The son, on the other hand, resents his father as an obstacle to his mother but does not resent his primary love object.

The Freudian formulation has a very different emphasis from that of the cognitive-developmental approach (see Chapter I), which postulates that identification is motivated by the need for self-identification, knowledge and competence. The Freudian theory stresses the emotional components of the identification process, which is lent tremendous impetus by the child's feelings about the object of its identification. A daughter who loves her mother will feel more pleasure in becoming like her than will a daughter who feels no such love.

Freud's explanation of the identification process suggests one respect in which the girl's identification with her mother may be a pleasant experience and one in which it may be unpleasant. The position of the mother as primary love object makes it pleasurable for the girl to identify with her. Mother was the source of good things early in life, and it well might make mother happy to see daughter becoming more like her. As the daughter grows older, is less nurtured by the mother and spends less time with her, she can still feel a closeness to her when she moves or speaks in similar fashion. Yet, according to Freud, part of the motivation for the girl to identify with her mother is fear of the mother. Thus the daughter may resent those of her mother's characteristics that she takes on.

They will remind her of her powerlessness and inadequacy ("I'm not really my mother, even though I'm trying to match her"), even while they satisfy her need for an identity. A daughter who is angry at her mother for coming between herself and her father does not cease to feel angry just because she grows to look, act and dress more like her mother. In fact, her anger may lead her to try to outdo her mother at being mother; she may try to beat her at her own game.

Penis Pity and Insufficient Nurturance

In the following paragraphs, I shall propose some modifications of Freud's theory about daughter-mother conflicts.

Penis Envy and Penis Pity

Horney (1966) and many others have suggested that it is not the penis itself that little girls envy. Rather, they say, it is the power that goes with being male in most societies, which, of course, includes the obvious political and economic power. Margaret Mead (1949) said in this context: "If parents define one child as less complete, less potentially gifted, with less right to be free, less claim to love and protection, or less a source of pride to themselves than the other, the child of that sex will, in many cases, feel envy." (p. 367) I want to suggest that girls' envy of boys also includes two other factors. These are (1) society's preference for males, which first appears in families as intense hopes that at least their first child will be male and which continues as the light in the parents' eyes as they regard their growing heir, and (2) the greater spectrum of active, energetic, risk-taking and achievement-oriented behavior that families allow and encourage in boys.

This envy of males often takes the form of girls wishing to be boys (one rarely sees the opposite). It is powerfully promoted (perhaps even entirely produced) by the cultural preference for and encouragement of boys, and one would be unnecessarily pessimistic, therefore, to consider penis envy universal and inevitable, a simple product of a physical difference. As a source of daughter-mother hostility, it appears to be capable of considerable modification by changes in the family and society.

Freud's theory and methodology make it easy to distort, misinterpret and exaggerate the behavior of the people studied. Although Freud shows by his own work that is important to take great care in interpreting behavior, all clinicians have blind spots and so caution can give way to the easier course of action: interpreting behavior to fit into a predetermined, supposedly universal schema. The part of his theory that allows one to make similar interpretations about apparently different phenomena appears throughout his writings but notably in his paper on negation (1925). From a practical standpoint, what it boils down to is that we are supposed to assume, for example, that all girls have penis envy. Thus if a girl says she wishes she had a penis, Freud takes this as an indication of her penis envy. Thus, also, if a girl says she is glad not to have a penis, Freud takes this as an indication that she is denying her penis envy. Perhaps more significantly, if a girl shows no sign of concern with the issue at all, Freud suggests the child is repressing her penis envy. His interpretation of boys' behavior as inevitably indicating castration anxiety is analogous. Indeed, it cannot be otherwise if one has decided that certain feelings are inevitably experienced by all girls or all boys.

Any theory that purports to apply to all people everywhere must include ways of transforming contradictory evidence into further "proof" of itself. Such twisting has some disturbing consequences. Once you accept a theory as true for everyone, the purpose of psychotherapy—indeed, the purpose of any two people exploring their experiences—is not to learn *what* is there but only to get a feeling for how strong, twisted or conscious are the things that you already "know" are there. The evidence for the universality of some things is more compelling than for others. With respect to penis envy, we need to ask whether there is some other, equally plausible interpretation. Or would an alternative interpretation explain some of Freud's observations while his own formulations explain others?

When we talk to both children and adults, males and females, we find evidence not only of some form of penis envy but also of what I shall call "penis pity": the attitude that penises are funny, strange-looking, wobbly, out of control, vulnerable to harm.

Freud believed that penis envy appears when very young girls first notice the physical differences between boys and themselves. Interestingly, around that same age (usually between two and four years) children have other important concerns that can give rise to penis pity.

About the time they discover the genital sex differences, children are being or have just been toilet-trained. This is the stage during which issues of control and self-control are paramount in the child's mind (Erikson, 1959). It is also a time when children's thinking is very concrete. In addition, children are then passing from the careless movements that can result in bodily injury toward a greater understanding of how to play without getting hurt, how to move about while still protecting their bodies. It is not surprising that little girls of this age may either show no signs of penis envy or, though envying the visibility and manipulability of the penis, may also experience a kind of penis pity. That is, they may regard themselves as lucky not to have to worry about trying to *control* an object that dangles and swings willy-nilly, or about trying to *protect* an object that is so external, sensitive and easily hurt, or about trying to *maintain privacy and avoid embarrassment* about visible, easily observable genitalia.

De Beauvoir (1974) suggested that for many little girls

this tiny bit of flesh hanging between boys' legs is insignificant or even laughable; it is a peculiarity that merges with that of clothes or haircut. Often it is first seen on a small newborn brother and, as Helene Deutsch puts it, "when the little girl is very young she is not impressed by the penis of her little brother." She cites the case of a girl of eighteen months who remained quite indifferent to it until much later, in accordance with her personal interests. It may even happen that the penis is considered to be an anomaly: an outgrowth, something vague that hangs, like wens, breasts, or warts; it can inspire disgust. (p. 307)

One woman recalled from her early childhood: "I remember sitting in the bathroom while my father took a shower talking to him. I thought his penis was ugly because of its shape and color. I was glad to be a girl because I was much prettier and didn't have one of those ugly dark dangling things." This memory is cited in *The Hite Report* (Hite, 1977) and is followed by Hite's observation: "Did you ever notice pornography always shows *erect* penises, not dangling ones?'' (p. 367)

Indeed, the male's genitals are more vulnerable to injury than the female's. In a *Time* magazine article (June 26, 1978), Dr. John Marshall, director of sports medicine at Manhattan's Hospital for Special Surgery and the trainer for Billie Jean King, is quoted as having said, ''A man's scrotum is much more vulnerable than a woman's ovaries. A woman's ovaries sit inside a great big sac of fluid—beautifully protected.'' (p. 60)

Freud was aware of the importance of the vulnerability of the penis. Much of the clinical material he cites to support the notion that boys fear castration and girls believe they have been castrated supports our theory that certainly girls, and probably also boys, feel some pity for the vulnerable penis. This may be either in addition to or instead of admiration. If, as Freud hypothesized, children are acutely aware of the vulnerability of the penis, and believe that its well-being is not entirely within the boy's control, then some phenomenon like penis pity would be expected to arise in many children of both sexes. While not claiming for penis pity either universality or a substantial role in child development, we do question whether it is necessary or reasonable to postulate a universal envy of the male genitalia.

Perhaps some girls feel penis pity, or perhaps all girls feel it more or less. Some girls learn to fear or desire penises because they learn early, for example, that their fathers are the rulers, or disciplinarians, in their families. But for others the awe, fear or desire of the penis does not develop until they learn more about men's greater economic political power or until they begin to develop relationships with boys in adolescence.

How does the notion of penis pity change our ideas about the potential for women's relationships with other women? If one believes only in penis envy, one has to assume that all daughters resent their mothers for not giving them penises, and that women feel contempt for themselves and for other women since they all lack this bodily part. The concept of penis envy suggests barriers between women that are inevitable and extremely difficult to surmount.

But once we accept the idea that penis envy is not inevitable and that little girls may sometimes feel quite relieved not to have an appendage that they consider worrisome, vulnerable, uncontrollable or even silly, this reason for daughters resenting their mothers and women believing all females are contemptible is no longer necessary.

Girls' "Insatiable" Need for Love Reexamined

We now consider Freud's observation that females need to be loved more than they need to love. Many myths echo this view, including the image of woman as ceaselessly demanding, nagging, wishing to drain men of their love, their seed, their independence, their self-respect. Then follow the myths that arise from the fear that women will succeed in those attempts: woman as witch, sorceress, Circe, Scylla and Charybdis, Cleopatra. In Ecclesiastes, woman is described as an ensnarer: "And I find more bitter than death the woman, whose heart ensnares and nets, and her hands as bands. . . ." But as these myths come to mind, so do other woman-myths: woman as earth-mother, Mother Nature, giver and protector of life. The former category of myths could be regarded as a consequence of the latter's exaggeration: the earth mother who requires a man's incessant sexual potency to continue conceiving, who smothers men and children with love and nurturance long after they have had enough, who uses the seductiveness of her warmth and sexuality to control men and children.

Women have sometimes been regarded in the same way leeches used to be when it was thought leeches could suck out, along with the blood, the poison in a human bloodstream and thus save lives. The image is of a woman who arranges for her life to revolve around a man, living to serve him so that he cannot imagine living (or living conveniently) without her, but in return demanding investments of time and emotion that he does not wish to make.

I want to suggest that an element of many relationships between mothers and daughters perpetuates such myths and helps to explain Freud's observation that women's needs for nurturance seem intense and perhaps "insatiable." It is simply this: the women who become nurturers/mothers often have been too little nurtured themselves as children. Such a situation reinforces the myths of both nurturant, altruistic Superwomen and demanding, never-satisfied evil goddesses. This same aspect in mother-daughter relationships often makes daughters *feel* that their needs for love are boundless and will never be met. We shall now examine in some detail how this develops.

The importance to society of women becoming mothers and thereby receiving respect (of a kind they have not been able to earn in any other capacity) is reflected in such phrases as "motherhood, the flag, and apple pie." This importance has been unquestioned, awe-inspiring, and is one reason for the harsh attacks on feminists who suggest changes in childrearing and parenting roles. It is also a reason for the paucity of discussion concerning issues treated in this book, since it calls into question the perfection of the timing, method and intensity that society chooses for teaching little girls to be mothers.

How does it come about that women are inadequately nurtured? A pattern occurs that is circular and self-perpetuating. Society gives families the task of training its young to behave in the socially approved ways. In North American society, this has usually meant that mothers were given this responsibility (see Dinnerstein, 1977). When children have not turned out "well," mothers have often been blamed—both by professional mental health workers and by society in general. In addition, women's roles have been limited and restricted. When we combine these factors with the breakdown of the extended family over the past hundred years, we see the following pattern: Mothers are given, and largely limited in function to, the task of raising children who behave in socially approved ways. Because of the limitations on what women can do, the mother's success or failure in accomplishing this task takes on intense importance; at the extreme (which is not so very rare), she and others measure her personal worth by how well she has accomplished it.

The isolation of housewives from each other (Friedan, 1963) and of families from each other (Mead, 1949) makes it difficult for mothers to know what is reasonably good mothering and to find support and companionship outside the home. They have long been taught that they are supposed to be serene, capable and happy as mothers, unruffled by whatever their children do, and that they are not supposed to want other substantial sources of enjoyment or company.*

Society gives mothers the task of teaching daughters to be nurturant and self-sacrificing, as they themselves are supposed to be. It is a natural outgrowth of this situation that, as part of her training in responding to the needs of others, the daughter of a lonely and insecure mother will be taught to meet the mother's needs as well. Insofar as the daughter tries to meet those needs, to that extent will her own needs for nurturance go unmet. Thus the daughter grows up feeling inadequately nurtured. When she becomes a mother, she will have unmet needs and may turn to her own daughter, hoping the daughter will meet them.

Daughters and mothers often collude in descriptions of this situation, such as "My mother is more of a friend to me than a mother," which seem acceptable and which sidestep the actual role reversal (daughter protecting and nurturing mother) that is taking place. In the *Diary of Anne Frank* (Frank, 1952), Anne says her mother cast her in the role of an equal rather than of a child who needed both nurturance and someone to look up to. Children often find it frightening when parents seem not to be strong but rather to need their children's friendship and support. Anne wrote: "I've grumbled a lot about Mummy, yet still tried to be nice to her again. Now it is suddenly clear to me what she lacks. Mummy herself has told us that she looked upon us more as her friends than her daughters. Now that is all very fine, but still, a friend can't take a mother's place. I need my mother as an example which I can follow. I want to be able to respect her. . . ." (p. 145)

One aspect of mother-daughter role reversal involves the daughter's knowledge that society expects her mother to be a good mother. Naturally, the daughter stands to gain more when her mother is relaxed than when she is angry or anxious. Therefore, the daughter begins to tell the public the story that her mother is just the kind of mother society wants. If her mother fails to bake

---

*In Bernard Slade's play *Same Time Next Year*, the female lead describes her behavior at a dinner party during the years when most of her time was spent raising her children. She relates how, as she talked with her husband's boss, she realized that she had been cutting up the meat on the man's plate, just as she had been used to doing for her children.

Halloween cookies for her to take to school, she does not complain or show her classmates her shame; she remains publicly silent, hoping no one will notice. Daughters who speak ill of their mothers in public, who suggest that their mothers are not ideal, must cope with the guilt of bringing shame and rejection on their mothers' heads. Since few children wish to carry this burden, daughters of inadequately nurturant or even normally nurturant women pretend their mothers are perfect; in some cases, at some level, they come to believe their own pretense. This lends a hollow quality to these daughters' attempts to mother and to nurture when they have children of their own.

Friday (1977) illustrates from her own experience how daughters at great cost to themselves will protect their mothers from knowledge they believe their mothers cannot handle. After a sexual encounter at age eighteen, Friday suspected she was pregnant. "It never occurred to me to call my mother. Mother was someone to whom I went when I was on top of the world. I couldn't bear to see anxiety in my mother; my remedy was for her never to see it in me. I circled the college infirmary on the hill, desperate to know the truth. . . ." (pp. 292–293) Daughters in upsetting situations believe their mothers are fragile, and they also believe their mothers regard them as fragile. By inhibiting their wish to turn to the mother for help, they protect what they believe to be their mother's weakness. Friday says she feared what people would think of her if they knew she had been sexually active at age eighteen. Given a choice of either acting on her need to confide in someone or protecting her mother from the disapproval of society ("You raised an immoral daughter; therefore, you are a bad mother"), she chose to protect her mother.

Mother-daughter role reversal is dramatically explored in two films that appeared in 1978: Ingmar Bergman's *Autumn Sonata* and Woody Allen's *Interiors*. Each film portrays a daughter who is intensely afraid of her mother's disapproval and yet anxious to nurture her mother. In *Autumn Sonata*, the daughter is still actively working for her mother's approval, whereas in *Interiors* some of the three daughters have begun to cope with the impossibility of winning that approval. In *Interiors*, the mother's neediness is apparent throughout the film, but in *Autumn Sonata* we see only toward the end of the film the full force of the mother's needs; in the latter, we also learn that the mother's wish to act out a role reversal began when her daughter was a very young child. The mother in *Autumn Sonata* says of a time when her daughter was tiny: "I wanted you to take care of me . . . put your arms around me and comfort me." And her daughter replies: "But I was only a child."

A number of converging factors frustrate the little girl's need for nurturance more than the little boy's. One is that the little girl is pushed into the nurturer's role unnecessarily early; this is reflected in society's delight in tiny girls who bring Daddy his slippers, help burn the roast for Daddy's dinner, etc., and its discouraging attitude toward boys who want to help with cooking or housework. Another factor is that the little girl often learns that society (often even her mother) values boys more than girls; this helps to shape her realistic belief that she is not loved as she would wish to be. Raphael (1978) quotes one woman who appears to have been struggling with her continuing sense of frustrated need: "I think I know what I can get and what I can't get from my mother, but I still go through periods of wanting *more*. I basically trust and love my mother very much, but I know she could never understand a lot of what's important to me. I've accepted that our relationship is limited, but I still feel a certain sadness." (p. 182)

The title of Griffin's article "On Wanting to Be the Mother I Wanted" (1977), reflects the way this pattern is perpetuated from one generation to the next. In the article, Griffin says, "I am angry at my mother for not mothering me." (p. 98) Rich (1976) writes, "Few women growing up in patriarchal society can feel mothered enough. The power of our mothers, whatever their love for us and their struggles on our behalf, is too restricted." (p. 243)

Society has developed an interesting method for encouraging its mothers to socialize their daughters in these ways. Stressing gender as an important classifying principle is the first step toward making it difficult for mother or daughter to admit that the mother may be psychologically harming her daughter. The reasoning goes something like this: "We're part of the same family, so I would never do anything to hurt her." And, still more powerful: "We are the girls of the family, and we girls always stick together."

Second, the fact that society discourages females from expressing anger makes it difficult for mothers to control their daughters' behavior through their anger. As de Sousa (1978) points out, women learn to label their own anger as "bitchiness," or shrewish behavior. This does not mean that mothers never yell at their daughters. What it does mean is that they feel far more comfortable using praise as a means to teach and control. Nietzsche's (1954) epigram "Praise is more obtrusive than a reproach" sums up this point. Suppose a mother yells at her daughter while telling her to quit playing baseball and come and serve her father his dinner. The daughter may easily learn to regard the order to serve dinner as unreasonable, because unreasonableness is consonant with the mother's yelling and anger. But if the mother asks sweetly and kisses and praises her for obedience, it is both cognitively and emotionally harder for the daughter to question the "rightness" of the order: cognitively, because of the dissonance between her mother's sweet manner and the fact that she is rigidly restricting her daughter's behavior; emotionally, because the mother's manner establishes the presumption that she is a "good" person, so the daughter will feel guilty about resenting her requests.

Mothers and daughters often appear to be very close, although the ambivalence or anger in their relationship can become so painful that both must deny it. What caretaking and nurturance the mother offers her daughter takes on a hollow, fantastic quality because of the anger and guilt that are denied or repressed. The more these "negative" aspects are denied, the more likely are mother and daughter to cover up those blotches with the flowery, storybook myth of the perfect closeness of their relationship.

When my daughter was born, I received a letter from a woman friend whose grown daughter was married and lived far away. The mother telephoned her daughter daily. The reason she gave for the frequent contact was her "close" relationship with the daughter. She not only concealed the frequency of these calls from her husband, however, but also became uneasy when talking about it. She seemed to sense that her behavior revealed her excessive dependence on her daughter. Her letter to me was a paean to the mother-daughter relationship. She wrote that while it is wonderful to have children at all, it is "our daughters" who are really special and close to us. The sex of my newborn daughter somehow destined our relationship to be a close one. The point of the letter was that we women could always count on our daughters. How much of her certainty came from the belief that a daughter would (even should) be taught to nurture her mother, be her company, take care of her?

To these considerations we add the known sex difference in need for approval (see Caplan, 1975, and Caplan, 1979, for a summary of this body of research). Society produces females who are more concerned than males about social approval. There might be a biologically based component to this as well, but no one yet knows. What has been determined is that we raise our females to look for approval and affection throughout life; we teach them that this is what girls are supposed to need. If one wants social approval, one tends to do the safest thing with respect to society. If one is female, the safest way to earn approval is to nurture (see Chapter III). So, given a firm basis of need for social approval, we train our daughters to grow into women who nurture and nurture, hoping that someday they will have done enough to win the approval they seek.

The needs that arise earliest in life, if unmet or inadequately met, tend to be experienced in a more pervasive, oceanic way than those that arise later. The need for nurturance is one of these. Since early needs were experienced before the infant or child could think in words or in abstract terms, the feelings related to them are often the hardest to pinpoint, describe and deal with. In contrast, needs that arise later in life are easier to bring under the person's conscious control and are easier to verbalize. These latter needs also arise when the person has greater ego strength, including both a more highly developed sense of differentiation between self and mother, and the abilities for taking action to meet one's own needs.

The need for nurturance is known to have devastating, even life-threatening effects if inadequately met. Though most women have not suffered life-threatening deprivation, the absence of adequate and unambivalent nurturance has intense and lasting consequences. These can be difficult to overcome in later life, even through psychotherapy, because they usually begin very early in life. The infant's and young child's helplessness in the face of unmet needs for nurturance often leads to rage at the person seen as having failed to meet those needs. This person is most likely the mother, and the rage, originating early, is intense. Though it is often unconscious, anyone who has seen a frightened or hungry infant's rage may imagine how the remnants of that rage can interfere when the infant grows up and is asked to offer others what was never received. It is like asking a starving woman to serve a feast. The mother's sense of her own early lack of nurturance, then, can make her feel angry and impatient when her daughter seems to need nurturance from her.

Freud's concept of fixation (1953) becomes relevant here. A child whose need at a crucial stage is unmet will thereafter have problems with that need. An infant who is underfed or overstuffed with food will probably have trouble with issues of eating—starving or overeating, for example—even as an adult; these problems will be likely to carry over more generally, producing an individual who seems "never to get enough" or who always feels empty. A woman, whose "destiny" is to nurture others, might well overdo or underdo her nurturing if she was inadequately nurtured as an infant and child, or if the nurturance was prematurely withdrawn. If this happened to her, then when she tries to offer nurturance to others she operates under substantial difficulty. Having been insufficiently nurtured, she may lack a sense of what is adequate, appropriate nurturance: she may offer too little, in keeping with her own experience, or she may offer too much or for too long.*

Taking this notion to its theoretical limits, within the Freudian framework, we can relate mothers' limited nurturing or withdrawal of nurturance to Freud'd theory of mourning. Freud suggested (1957) that when people die, those who loved them may try to hold on to the deceased by "introjecting the lost object," trying to become more like them. If we can assume that loss of or decrease in the mother's nurturance is like a partial death to the daughter,

---

*The most dramatic modern demonstration of the frustration and uncertainty most women experience is reported in Friedan's *The Feminine Mystique* (1963). Friedan explains that a "women's magazine" each month asked its readers to write to them about some issue. One month in 1960, the topic was "Why Young Mothers Feel Trapped." At this time, the media were touting the image of the "happy housewife" who was delighted to stay at home tending the house and children. According to Friedan, 24,000 replies to this question poured in, so many that "the editors were shocked." One thing the letters made clear was the isolation of each woman from others in similar positions. Each read the newspapers and the women's magazines and believed what she read. Each unhappy woman had been afraid she was abnormal, "crazy," unusually demanding and ungrateful, and therefore each had kept her unhappiness to herself.

we can hypothesize that daughters would feel more reluctant to live differently from their mothers than sons from their fathers, because the daughters would have been more involved in the introjection process. This would encourage the self-perpetuating pattern of women's role limitations, the common assertion that women help sustain the oppression of women.

Much of the theory about the difficulties between mothers and daughters has taken as a basis the assumption that the "oceanic feeling" said to be experienced by the infant *in utero* is desirable and pleasurable. Freud proposed that the wish to return to the womb is an important search for pleasure, and Dinnerstein (1977) has recently discussed the idea. In a time of stress, people may wish for cessation of pain and increase in pleasure, as well as to be taken care of instead of constantly striving to cope. Yet we cannot assume that this is a wish to return to the womb or to the original symbiosis with the mother.

At the very least, we must consider the possibility of another innately determined motivating factor that makes independence, achievement and coping desirable and pleasurable to humans. White (1959) called this competence motivation. Since becoming independent and learning to cope are essential to survival of the species, it is possible that such motivation might be inborn. In addition, if we are to assume that natural and early experiences are pleasurable for infants, we must consider the newborn colt's struggle to stand on its own an early and pleasurable experience, one that would be desirable to repeat in varied forms. Similar logic would apply to the newborn human infant struggling to take its first breath.

Early foundations are laid for the daughter to become happily strong, competent and independent, and the mother usually participates in these: they break into a smile when a six-week-old daughter first smiles, they help the young child learn to walk. Here, the mother is encouraging her daughter's growth, not smothering her increasing separateness, and it is only in the most extreme pathological cases that mothers do not do such positive things at all. Therefore, it is probably misleading to attribute conflicts between daughter and mother extensively to their presumably basic need to merge into each other. One would want to cite very early developmental history as a cause of emotional and interpersonal difficulty only if one were certain that this was a cause, since the earliest events are the ones that are hardest to change. In addition, proponents of continued restriction of women's roles have often justified their own rigidity by asserting that "mothers and daughters cannot see themselves as separate people and do not wish to do so." (The phrase carries echoes of "Black people don't *want* to go to school with whites" and "Poor people are just poor because they are too lazy to work.") It is quite a different matter to consider what later life events might throw mother and daughter together in an uneasy alliance as an adjustment to unreasonable social restrictions.

How is the daughter shaped into the nurturant role? One good way for learning to take place is through practice and reward for doing the task correctly. To oversimplify, a mother who wants to teach her daughter to become a "properly" nurturant female must encourage her to practice such behavior. Since sex-differential socialization begins during the first years of life, the mother cannot spend all her time nurturing a daughter who must practice *being* the nurturer. If only the two of them are home, the mother may even teach the daughter how to take care of her. If there are other children, or when the father is home, the mother can show the daughter how to take care of them. But time spent by the daughter giving nurturance is time that the mother cannot spend nurturing her.

Naturally, one would not have mothers spend all day and night nurturing children. Children need to sleep, cry, play, rest. The question concerns the proportion of time spent in the teaching of nurturing, compared to other activities of the child. A little girl who is regarded as "needing to learn" to nurture will practice such activities in play as well, taking care of younger siblings, friends and dolls. Her wishes to run, yell, climb trees, roll in the mud, will be dampened as she is either punished for such activities or more subtly told that "little girls aren't supposed to." The little boy is less likely to spend time helping out, taking care of others, because such behavior is not encouraged, sometimes not even rewarded, and often discouraged: "You don't have to do that for Mommy," says the anxious mother or father who fears the boy will become effeminate. In addition, the little boy will spend time running, yelling, climbing trees, rolling in the mud, and will be less likely as he grows older to spend time taking care of dolls and stuffed animals.

When a baby comes to visit, a very young girl will be encouraged to look at, talk to, hold the baby, but a very young boy will probably not be so encouraged. As they grow older, and as older children come to visit, the daughter of the house is more likely than the son to "take care of" the visiting children. When Mommy and Daddy have company, the daughter will be asked to serve the hors d'oeuvres. Thus a girl spends more time per se in learning to nurture and also has a more restricted range of other activities that are consistent with her "appropriate" sex-role behavior. She is likely to believe "I know who I am as long as I keep nurturing," while the boy learns to feel that he can engage in a wide range of activities and still be "all boy."

Bowlby (1978) has written that some people can form close relationships only if they take the role of "caretaker." He observes that such people are far more likely to be girls and women than boys and men. In explaining how this comes to be, he says that people who are comfortable only when taking care of others were probably placed in the role of caretaker by one or both parents when very young. This adds force to the notion that girls are younger and more often asked to take a nurturant role toward at least one parent, possibly both, and likely the siblings as well.*

---

*There are many examples of cross-cultural similarity in the role of women as nurturers. Bernard (1974) offers the following description of the Rajputs of India:

. . . during the months when the baby is too old to lie quietly on a cot and too young to walk itself, it is, if possible, turned over to an older girl to carry when the mother is busy working. As a rule, this caretaker will be an older sister, but a cousin may take the child if the sisters-in-law are on good terms." And among the residents of Tarong, in the Philippines: ". . . in no household did a mother have sole responsibility for her children—it would be unthinkable. . . . If the house is relatively isolated and the family nuclear, the father may well hold the baby whenever he is not in the fields, bathe it, change its clothes, feed it tidbits. If the house has many women or older girls, he will rarely do more than play with the child while it is still young. (p. 7, quoted from *Six Cultures, Studies of Child Rearing*, edited by Beatrice Whiting, 1974)

Neisser (1973) writes of the Hopi Indians:

If there is an older sister (a five-year-old qualifies as old enough), she will be entrusted with much of the baby's care under her mother's supervision as soon as he is a few months old. She carries the baby on her back as she goes

Since in some ways women are infantilized, treated as children, how can it be that girl children are not nurtured as much or as long as little boys? How can it be that the infantilized sex receives less nurturance?

There are at least two levels of socialization. One is the superficial level of manner and gesture; another is the deeper level of identity and role. At the level of manner and gesture are such examples as men opening doors for women and not discussing business with them, and women expressing opinions only rarely and with apologies, hesitations and qualifications. At the level of identity and role is the assumption that females are supposed to nurture males: to cook for them, listen to their troubles while suppressing their own needs to express their own frustrations, give and renew the strength of men so the latter can shape the institutions that are publicly said to change the world.

It is known that parents and teachers tend to treat girl and boy children differently, and by the time they reach preschool age differences are found in their basic attitudes toward other people.

---

about the village playing and performing the numerous tasks that fall to her lot. These child nurses are not merely "helping." They are doing the actual work of caring for a baby, and there is nothing elective about their job. (p. 313)

And of the girls among the Ifaluk people in the Pacific, Neisser (1973) writes:

A seven- or eight-year-old cooks, cares for the younger children, collects flowers, and is introduced by her mother to the activities which provide the family with food and clothing. Girls have more responsibility for carrying on the business of daily living than do boys, and consequently spend more time with their mothers. When a group of children play together the eight and nine-year-old girls will supervise them and incidentally teach them how they are supposed to behave and what is considered proper on the island. When a girl puts on a grass skirt, she becomes a deputy for her mother and is expected, among other duties, to be hospitable to guests. (p. 338)

Within the Gusii tribe of Kenya (Neisser, 1973), "the oldest among the uninitiated girls, the seven- or eight-year-old, is left in charge of the house and the younger children when the mother and the older girls go out to work in the fields." (p. 345)

Lynn (1974) describes how, in Mexican-American families, in the event of the mother's illness, the eldest daughter is expected to take charge of all household tasks. He notes that the mother gives her baby daughters more attention than her sons, but after the first year her daughters are reared more severely than her sons.

From very early in life, girls are taught to be sensitive to the feelings and needs of other people. This is a first step toward the nurturer's role: in order to take care of someone's needs, one must first know what those needs are, and the best possible nurturer will even sense the other person's needs before being told.

Research about sex differences (Caplan, 1975; Caplan, 1979) has shown that in the presence of an adult, little girls usually behave less aggressively than when they think no one is around, whereas this is not true of little boys. The presence of an adult also increases the likelihood that little girls will behave in altruistic ways (Caplan, 1973), but does not have that effect on little boys. This is typical of the research in the field. Little girls become sensitive and responsive to the opinions and needs of others from very early in life.

The same pattern continues through childhood and adolescence. A fifteen-year-old female patient said that her idea of heaven was the weekend she spent alone with her boyfriend at his house. When asked what was the best part of the weekend, a dreamy expression appeared in her eyes, and she said, "On Sunday morning, Bob cooked breakfast and made a mess in the kitchen, and I got to clean it up." The same patient, having been badly treated by her father and having seen him similarly treat her mother and siblings, was extremely worried when the possibility arose of her parents' separating. She said, "He can't even open a can of beans. How will he eat?"

This typifies the attitude of women that men are "little boys who cannot take care of themselves." The corollary is that women and girls should take care of these men. As De Beauvoir (1964) says, in our society it is mostly men who do the business of the world, struggling and working in what they call the "jungle" of business and the "torments" of arts. What is left for women is to restore and nourish these creatures who so exhaust themselves by daily toil.

We understand how early the sex-role differentiation with respect to nurturance begins when we consider the reactions of most people to the situation described above. Reading about the patient cleaning up the kitchen after her boyfriend, one may feel concerned about a girl who finds her value in such activities; one may even feel angry with a society and family that encourage such an attitude. But one is unlikely to feel the immediate uneasiness that reading the same story about a teenaged boy would probably evoke. Similarly, one who hears that a girl toddler brings her father his slippers may consider this appropriate or may even think she should not have to learn such behavior. Again, however, most people are unlikely to feel the instant inclination to regard her as weird or strange that they would feel upon hearing that a little boy did the same thing.

Even when picturing such behavior on the part of boys, one is likely to imagine them with facial expressions and thoughts in their minds different from those that girls would have. Most people would imagine the male child and male teenager as "helping out, doing a favor, showing a little consideration," with serious or even kind expressions on their faces. The little girl and the teenaged girl, on the other hand, would be imagined as looking hopeful for approval and appreciation, since they know that this is the way to fit into the role of "female." The boy and young man know that "what really matters" about being male is what they do at work, though they may "help out" with the tasks of nurturing, but the growing female learns increasingly that being female *is* in large part being nurturant. And, as noted, it is primarily from her mother that a daughter learns to fill the nurturant role.

According to Belotti (1975), mothers are tolerant of baby boys' rituals and requirements at mealtime but insist on quick and unfussy eating by girls. Belotti points out that girls are usually weaned earlier than boys, a practice that seems to be related to a greater comfort in keeping boys dependent on mothers. She notes that mothers begin toilet training earlier for girls than for boys, and are less tolerant of dirtiness in their girls, so that they are requiring more self-control, more adult and less troublesome behavior on the part of their daughters. In effect, mothers teach their daughters the following: "Everything is fine as long as I have to do as little as possible for you, so hurry up and learn how to fend for yourself" (p. 40). Elsewhere, Belotti says that girls are used to "sacrificing themselves from a very early age" (p. 32), having been taught to do so by their mothers.

In 1845, Sigourney wrote about the relative difficulties involved in raising sons and daughters. Her attitude expresses much of what remains typical in mothers' treatment of their sons:

In the discipline of sons, mothers need a double portion of the wisdom that is from above. Let them ever keep in view the different spheres of action allotted to the sexes. What they blame as obstinacy, may be but that firmness, and fixedness of purpose, which will hereafter be needed to overcome the obstacles of their adventurous course. Perhaps, it is hardly to be expected that they should be reduced to the full degree of feminine subordination, any more than inured to the routine of domestic employment. (p. 126)

Needless to say, Sigourney did not advise mothers to allow their daughters such "firmness" or freedom from "the full degree of feminine subordination."

The difference in how the sexes are reared has another consequence besides producing nurturant girls and less nurturant boys. The growing girl comes to notice that her parents treat her brother differently from the way they treat her. She may observe that they set fewer limits on his behavior and make fewer demands that he take care of others and behave in a "proper" way. From the time they are toddlers, comparing the levels of the milk in their respective glasses to see whether their mother gave one a little more than the other, children are sensitive to differences in what one parent does for them compared to their siblings. In addition, they often interpret "different" as "better" or "worse." The mother treats her daughter differently from her son, and the daughter may interpret this as indicating that her mother loves her more or loves her less. When she learns that parents and society consider boys more valuable than girls, the daughter becomes convinced that being treated differently from her brother means being treated "worse."

She is then in the following predicament: if she stops doing what her parents want, she risks losing their love and eliciting their disapproval; if she remains within the arena of "girl-appropriate" behavior, she avoids the risk of losing their love but at the same time still feels less valued than her male sibling. Even very young people like to feel highly regarded, and when treated as inferiors they nevertheless strive for esteem. Within their limited range of acceptable behavior, then, little girls often are left with only one alternative: not only can they continue that acceptable behavior, but they can do it with ever-increasing intensity and frequency. Some research (see Caplan, 1974, for a review) demonstrates how this principle operates within the classroom. Elementary school girls who fail academically tend to show increased "prosocial" behavior. That is, keeping within the limits of socially approved female behavior, they simply spend more time and energy upholding the teacher's standards for good behavior: they hand out pencils, "tell" on misbehaving children, and so on. Thus the social goal of training daughters to help out and protect society's standards is furthered.

The daughter grows into the role of nurturer. She sacrifices her wish to be nurtured, because it is "inappropriate" for girls, in favor of taking on a nurturant role, hoping to win some approval.

It is clear that the interaction of the rules of society with the emotional needs of individuals is producing many women whose needs for love and nurturance seem immense. Let us consider whether the principles of evolutionary theory would suggest that these feelings are inevitable.

If one were to look for behavior that contributes to the survival of the species, it would not make sense to believe that women must have an unmeetable need for affection. In fact, quite the opposite might be true. If females were really intended to become the nurturers of the race, a sensible belief would be that their need for nurturance is limited in time and quantity. It would be inconvenient to the survival of the species if the intended nurturers were so burdened with their own needs for nurturance that they could not nurture others.

For the sake of argument, let us assert that the survival of species requires that girls be nurturers. Yet suppose the innately determined pattern is that girls have an unmeetable need for affection when very young, but this need conveniently decreases around puberty so that they are then free to become nurturant. In that case, we would have to wonder why society begins so early to stream the sexes into their roles. A girl pushed by her parents and society into the role of nurturer, and *out* of the role of nurtured, may feel cut off too soon from her family's nurturance. We know that such a premature cessation in the meeting of a child's needs makes those needs seem even more intense. In addition, if we wish to make the girl happy in accepting the role of nurturer, it might make more sense to keep her in the role of nurtured until she can consider the possible compensations (e.g., a baby) imminent, or at least comprehensible and meaningful. Indeed, Bowlby (1969) studied the beginnings of nurturant behavior in very young children of both sexes and demonstrated that children are not naturally prepared to continue it consistently and conscientiously:

> Another example of typical items of instinctive behavior occurring in the immature but in sequences insufficiently organized for the unit to be functional is the maternal behavior of little girls, and sometimes also of little boys. For a longish period a child of three may act in a typically maternal way towards a doll, or even towards a real baby. Then something distracts her, the maternal behavior ends abruptly, and for a long stretch of time the doll, or baby, is left neglected. (p. 159)

Nevertheless, most societies try to teach their young girls to act consistently in a nurturant, caretaking way (see Chapter III).

Bowlby (1969) describes problems that arise when people are forced to behave prematurely in ways that will become useful or pleasurable later on, when they can fully enjoy the fruits of their endeavors. He shows how bits of play, such as caring for dolls, may imitate portions of eventual adult roles. These bits of behavior become "reorganized more as a plan with a set-goal" (p. 160) and take on different emotional significance later in life. We can understand the harm that comes from premature pushing of children into adult behavior (in which the goals are still unavailable to them) if we think of the analogy of sexual behavior. Children do not have their own real infants, just as they are not capable of becoming pregnant, and so caretaking behavior and sexual activity do not have the same goals then as they would when they are older. Both nurturant behavior and sexual behavior can, of course, involve pleasures apart from the above-named goals. But neither activity is pleasurable if it is imposed, and neither is pleasant if one feels inadequate and unprepared for it. Children are neither psychologically nor physically prepared to take major responsibilities for nurturing other people, and forcing them to do so causes known psychological damage. This damage is most often referred to in laypersons' terms as being deprived of childhood, but social stereotyping has made it more acceptable in the case of little girls.

CHAPTER 3

Barriers between Women

This chapter discusses some of the common sources of barriers that can arise between females in many different kinds of relationships. Some of the material has been mentioned in earlier chapters but will be expanded here. Other sources that apply with particular force to the mother-daughter relationship will be discussed in Chapter IV.

Woman as Nurturer

Little girls learn early that they are supposed to become nurturant and supportive creatures. Little boys are not taught that a nurturant role is essential to their gender. Bardwick and Douvan (1971) have described the characteristics that make a woman most successful in family roles as including "the capacity . . . to sustain and support members of the family rather than pursuing her own goals, to enhance relationships through boundary-less empathy . . . ." (p. 236)

De Beauvoir (1974) reviews the woman-as-nurturer images in history and literature. Having cited them as they have been applied to mothers, she writes:

> Yet close behind the sainted Mother presses the throng of female white magicians who offer for man's use the juices of herbs and the radiations of the stars: grandmothers, old women with kindly eyes, goodhearted servants, Sisters of Mercy, nurses with wonderfully gentle hands, the loved one of Verlaine's dream.
> Sweet, pensive and dark and surprised at nothing,
> And who at times will kiss you on the forehead like a child.

She continues:

> To them is ascribed the pure mystery of gnarled vine and fresh water, they dress and heal wounds; their wisdom is the silent wis-

dom of life, they understand without words. . . . Sisters, childhood
friends, pure young girls, all the mothers of the future belong to this
beneficent band. (p. 197)

Women's nurturant behavior has often been misinterpreted as a
failure of women to consider themselves separate from other people. Hammer (1976, pp. 14–15) says of daughters that "to some
extent they never achieve a clear sense of a separate [from mother]
self at all." Of mothers she says that the "tendency to live in and
through other people—to behave as though there were no difference between self and other—is an essential part of being a good
mother."

The type of mothering Hammer describes has nightmarish qualities and consequences, and one would not wish to hold it up as
desirable. As a writer who is not a psychologist, she seems to have
mistaken either the mother's wish to take credit for the accom-
plishment of her children, or her projection of her own feelings
onto her children for a deficient or absent sense of a separate self.
Some such deficiency no doubt exists in some mothers and some
daughters. But a mother may clearly separate herself from others,
even though her lack of self-confidence and society's limitations on
what mothers may achieve in their own right lead her to believe
that she must devote all her energies to helping her children.

Another distinction must be made. The failure to regard oneself
as separate from others is an extremely serious psychological disturbance that is very rare. What Hammer perhaps meant to refer to
was the frequency with which mothers suppress their own feelings
and wishes in order to meet the needs of others. To meet the needs
of others successfully, it is important to be able to separate oneself
from them. One who cannot understand this separateness does not
meet the needs of others; one assumes that one's own needs are
the same as theirs. Thus successful nurturing involves a substantial
degree of psychological separation of self from others. Though a
mother may come to suppress her own needs and feelings so automatically that she begins to lose sight of what they really are, this
does not necessarily decrease her sensitivity to her children's
needs. What she suppresses and, later, represses may interfere
with her attempts to meet their needs, but this is different from
having no sense of separateness. In fact, many such mothers feel
increasingly empty and inadequate while regarding the children as

progressively more wonderful and awe-inspiring; this increases not only the mother's sense of being separate from them but also her sense of being unworthy of them. It is important to keep in mind that absence of a separateness is not the same thing as fulfilment of the nurturant role.

Harriet Lerner (1977) writes: "Women have been taught that they must be non-threatening help-mates and ego-builders to men, lest men feel castrated and emasculated." (p. 7) Dinnerstein (1977) observes that women are "seen as naturally fit to nurture other people's individuality; as the born audience in whose awareness other people's subjective existence can be mirrored; as the being so peculiarly needed to confirm other people's worth, power, significance that if she fails to render them this service she is a monster, anomalous and useless." (p. 112)

Belotti (1975) notes that girls, compared to boys, are supposed to "more affectionate, more grateful, sweet and playful, more fun to dress, company in the home (nobody expects a boy to be company), a help with the housework. . . ." (p. 128) Her point about the girl being "company in the home" reflects the theme that the little girl is even supposed to meet some of her mother's emotional needs, to nurture her. Belotti later says that women "are conditioned, and few can escape it, to think that it is the duty of a woman, whether she be daughter, wife or mother, to put herself in the service of the male and not neglect the least of his needs. Girls . . . are used to sacrificing themselves from a very early age." (p. 32) She writes further:

> The conditioning of little girls towards serving boys and adults in general, as well as the pressure exerted on them so that their affection is never distracted but rather directed towards resolving banal practical problems, displaces an important part of their vital energy. Rather than engaging in games, creative enterprise, or free activity which might be an end in itself and result in fulfillment of their own personality, they are kept busy with activities which serve the group as a whole. (p. 135)

Reeves (1971) assembled a series of readings across a wide span of history that illustrate the way females have been expected to fill the nurturant, supportive role. She says: "The traditional model postulates that woman is primarily homemaker, wife, and mother;

that her qualities are nurturing and passive; that she is destined to inhabit the private as her exclusive sphere." (p. 155) As an example, she quotes Martin Luther, writing in 1566:

> "A woman is, or at least should be, a friendly, courteous, and a merry companion in life, whence they are named, by the Holy Ghost, househonours, the honour and ornament of the house, and inclined to tenderness, for there unto are they chiefly created, to bear children, and be the pleasure, joy and solace of their husbands." (p. 99)

Reeves also cites Charles Butler's book *The American Lady* (1839), in which the following passages occur as descriptions of "the effects which the influence of the female character produces":

> "It is not like the periodical inundation of a river, which overspreads once in a year a desert with transient plenty. It is like the dew of heaven which descends at all seasons, returns after short intervals, and permanently nourishes every herb of the field. . . . It is accordingly manifest, that, in sprightliness and vivacity, quickness of perception, in fertility of invention, in powers adapted to unbend the brow of the learned, to refresh the overlaboured faculties of the wise, and to diffuse throughout the family circle the enlivening and endearing smile of cheerfulness, the superiority of the female mind is unrivalled." (p. 160)

In offering some modern examples, Reeves includes the following from Fromm (1956): "The masculine character can be defined as having the qualities of penetration, guidance, activity, discipline, and adventurousness; the feminine character by the qualities of productive receptiveness, protection, realism, endurance, motherliness." (p. 100)

Reeves (1971) describes what happens to role division in families whose men are unemployed: "The women's roles didn't contract; they expanded. Not only did the wife have to go on with the household routine—cooking, cleaning, taking care of the children—but frequently the wife was also the one who held the family together when her husband was prone to go to pieces." (p. 197). And: ". . . the men . . . drifted helplessly and apathetically in the streets, looking dully for some means of rescue. On the other hand, the woman's world—the world of cooking, cleaning, mending, and childrearing—remained intact.'' In yet another instance: ''With unemployed miners unable to get other work—and unwilling to work in nearby textile mills because they considered that they would have to do woman's work—their wives have become the chief breadwinners in the family. But according to Dorothy Cohen, executive director of the Family Services Association of Wyoming Valley, Pennsylvania, there's no real role reversal: 'In many instances, the women are faced with carrying the responsibility for home and children in addition to their jobs. Often, the care of the children is haphazard. Sometimes, relatives help. Day-care facilities are almost completely lacking in Wyoming Valley.' '' (p. 197)

It is striking in the last example that, rather than the husbands taking over the child care, it is left to relatives, day-care centers or ''haphazard'' means. Women can be either nurturers, or nurturers *and* breadwinners. But men tend to be very reluctant to become nurturers, especially if that is ''all'' that they are supposed to do.

A July 1978 Neilsen survey of currently married working mothers of all socioeconomic groups indicated that only 15 percent of the husbands helped with household tasks (though 23 percent had children who helped out). Nielsen executive John C. Stermer commented, ''The husband helps only to a minor degree—with bill paying, chauffeuring, and child rearing.''

Gerda Lerner (1977) has provided an historical survey that bears out the female-as-nurturer role across the span of American history. Comparing woman's to man's role, she writes: ''*He* was to express himself in his work and, through it and social action, was to help transform his environment; *her* individual growth and choices were restricted to lead her to express herself through love, wifehood, and motherhood—through the support and nurture of others, who would act for her.'' (p. xxvi)

Writing specifically of nineteenth-century America, she notes:

For American boys the development of a strong individuality and strong will was a necessary value, preparing them for their life roles. For girls the subduing of the will, the acceptance of self-abnegation, and the development of excessive altruism were the desired educational goals. Fathers as different as the educational radical Bronson Alcott, the upper-class conservative George Palmer Putnam, and the anonymous fathers or the masters of the slave girls all strove to mold their daughters into this pattern. Interestingly, mothers as different as the reformer Martha Wright, the quiet, domestic mother of Francis Willard, and the anonymous mother of Rose Schneiderman, who toiled in a sweat-shop to support her orphaned children, participated in this indoctrination, which seemed to them to be in the best interest of their daughters.

Therefore, she points out, "A girl's childhood would bring the usual joys, strains, and stresses, but more frequently than the boy she would experience growing up as a loss, confinement, a decrease of freedom." (p. xxvi)

In a review of woman's roles from colonial times to the present, Ryan (1975) demonstrated how extensively woman's appropriate functions were thought to fall into the category of nurturance. In the eighteenth century, women of the upper classes "were instructed to render unto their spouses their entire stock of love, warmth, and solace." (p. 114) In the nineteenth century, "whether the women of industrial society remained ever secluded in the home or spent a few years in the lowest ranks of the work force, their sex was identified primarily with specialized domestic functions, supplying the immediate physical and emotional needs of husbands and children. The quintessential standard of femininity became nurturance, first of individual families and through them all of America." (p. 13) Ryan further points out that "woman's obligation to honour and comfort her husband was clearly designed to insure order in the social unit of the family" (p. 39).

Even female education, Ryan notes, was "preparatory to altruism rather than personal achievement," and women were taught to make it part of their duty to please, and "to cultivate the habit of making others happy daily." (p. 150) In return for serving a husband "faithfully in the backstage of American life, without power, status, or achievement of her own," a major consolation was supposed to be the hope of "being paramount in one heart" (p. 154), and hence the ideal of romantic love as the rationale for marriage was strengthened.

Ryan (1975) cites a nineteenth-century writer, Donald Mitchell, who articulated the domestic fantasy that a wife was to fulfill: "Your wants are all anticipated: the fire is burning brightly; the clean hearth flashes under the joyous blaze. . . . If trouble comes upon you, she knows that her voice, beguiling you into cheerfulness, will lay aside your fears." (pp. 154–55)

In a book called *Letters to Mothers* (1845), a popular author of the time, Lydia Howard Sigourney, suggested how mothers should raise their daughters:

> Inspire her with a desire to make all around her, comfortable and happy. Instruct her in the rudiments of that science, whose results are so beautiful. Teach her, that not selfish gratification, but the good of a household, the improvement of even the humblest dependent, is the business of her sex. . . . Especially, if you visit the aged, or go on errands of mercy to the sick and poor, let her be your companion. Allow her to sit by the side of the sufferer, and learn those nursing services which afford relief to pain. (p. 124)

By the mid- to late nineteenth century, social Darwinists had alleged that woman's physical equipment rendered her "by nature the more social sex, formed to nurture and serve the race, rather than to scrap and fight for personal gain" (Ryan, 1975, p. 226). At the end of the nineteenth and beginning of the twentieth centuries, as they became more active outside the home, women formed and ran organizations the avowed goals of which "remained altruistic: to serve the needy and weak rather than to conquer wealth and power for the female sex." (p. 232)

Not only in his theory but also in his personal life, Freud (cited in Smith, 1978, p. 47) believed that the nurturant role was the best, most proper role for women. Discussing his future mother-in-law, Freud wrote in a letter:

> I do not think I am being unfair to her; I see her as a person of great mental and moral power standing in our midst, capable of high accomplishments, without a trace of the absurd weaknesses of old women, but there is no denying that she is taking a line against us all, like an old man. Because her charm and vitality have lasted so long, she still demands in return her full share of life—not the share of old age—and expects to be the center, the ruler, an end in herself. Every *man* who has grown old honorably wants the same, only in a woman one is not used to it. As a mother she ought to be content to know that her three children are fairly happy, and she ought to sacrifice her wishes to their needs.

Smith (1978, p. 30), cites what may be the most grotesque example of the self-sacrificing mother image. She says it originated as a Chinese tale thousands of years old and quotes an English version:

There was a young man loved a maid
Who taunted him: "Are you afraid,"
She asked, "to bring me today
Your mother's heart upon a tray?"

He went and slew his mother dead;
Tore from her breast her heart so red,
Then towards his lady love he raced
But tripped and fell in all his haste.

As the heart rolled on the ground
It gave forth a plaintive sound.
And it spoke, in accents mild:
"Did you hurt yourself, my child?"

Jungian analyst Irene Claremont de Castillejo wrote (1973) that
the basic feminine attitude "is more nearly an attitude of acceptance, an awareness of the unity of all life and a readiness for
relationships." (p. 15) She further wrote of "woman's fundamen-
tal role of helping [man] to find himself . . . and woman's attitude of
spiritual waiting, and tending, and readiness for the meeting with
its opposite which is a prerequisite for inner wholeness." (p. 56)
She promises of woman: "But if she can hold the oil ready within
the lamp, then, when the masculine spark comes, there burns a
flame which is alive, and lights our human world." (p. 57) She
divides women into three types: the maternal, the hetaera and the
mediumistic. The maternal type's role is to "care for and protect
whatever is new and growing in the man, if it enhances his position
or influence in *outer* life, as such things are important in his role of
husband and father to the children." The hetaera type's value lies
in providing "inspiration and flattery" to her man. The mediumistic type "renders the unique service to man of mediating to him the
contents of the collective unconscious. . . . Indeed it is vitally
important for a woman who is to handle images from the collective
unconscious to have a strong ego, if she is not to get lost in its
mazes and cause confusion to herself and those around her." (pp.
56–69) The reason for women to be strong, then, is so they can
better support and help their men. In this connection, Claremont
de Castillejo points out that women often regard men as little boys,
in need of care, though the converse is not often true. In summary,

she says that woman needs to give *in order not to feel empty.*
"Woman needs to give. She cannot help herself. . . . This flow of
life is not intended only for her children but also for her mate. . . ."
Woman's primal driving force, she says, is "love and the service of
those she loves." (pp. 149–54)

Rowbotham (1973), on the other hand, describes the way the
long-term strains of that nurturant role in fact *produce* a feeling of
emptiness:

> Housework can never be a normal job routine because emotion
> erupts in its midst. Crisis and turmoil mean that the woman has to
> drop everything and put Humpty together again. Friends phone,
> children run home screaming, the husband glowers behind his paper,
> the woman retreats behind a barrier of elaborate calm. Brought up to
> feel that she must keep things going, patch and cover up, settle
> everyone down, she absorbs the tension magically within herself
> until it is no longer evident. The original barrier becomes a case
> between her and the world, the case hardens, the violence she has
> contained ravages her. She begins to feel completely hollow. (p. 73)

The "neurosis of nothingness," Rowbotham says, comes from the
nature of the work women are raised to do at home, in which they
learn to feel that they are truly women only if they are self-
denying:

> Self-affirmation can only come through self-abnegation. The "fem-
> inine" woman, the good mother, can only realize herself by pouring
> herself into her husband and children. Female conditioning into self-
> denying service means that women even with relatively high earn-
> ings drop into looking after men. . . . A friend of mine who is a dental
> receptionist used to wash the dentist's shirts. All this is . . . because
> by doing these tasks . . . women at work are subtly flattered that their
> sex is recognized. (p. 76)

Sheehy (1976) points out how the woman-as-nurturer ideal supports the sexual double standard. She suggests that the double
standard has developed and persisted partly because the "delayed
blooming myth" of female sexuality, the idea that women are not
very much interested in sex, makes it possible for females to sub-
ordinate their sexual needs (their desires to have their own needs
met) to the nurturing and building up of the ego of their men.

Illustrating the potentially disastrous consequences of the nurturant role, Sheehy (1976) tells the story of a woman who, at age thirty-eight, feeling she had spent much of her life taking care of other people, and wishing for someone to take care of her, comes to the brink of suicide, thinking, "Where is it written that women are the only nurturers?"

The Cinderella story may be the most familiar expression of nurturance presented as a womanly ideal. Cinderella's goodness is pointed out by contrasting her unhappiness, suffering, deprivation and toiling for others with her stepsisters' laziness, self-indulgence and spending of time and energy on their outward appearance. The latter are drawn as ugly; Cinderella is usually drawn as pretty, even in her rags. The implication, however, is that it is her suffering that earns her the right to a fairy godmother, and by that route she comes to appear captivatingly beautiful.

The story of Snow White and the Seven Dwarfs is another fairy tale representation of this role. Snow White, in becoming a woman ready for marriage, must take care of seven little men. That they are little men makes her work good practice for nurturing both husband and children. Like most Western housewives, she does the work alone, isolated. Not only is she encouraged to perform these nurturing, housekeeping services in return for a roof over her head, but indeed it is the major activity she is given in the story. For the rest, when her work is done, it is not by singing, dancing or writing fairy tales that she wins her prince, but by lying back passively and being beautiful to look at, so the prince can take the active role in their relationship.

Recent books that offer advice on the mother-daughter relationship, such as Neisser's *Mothers and Daughters* (1973), point out the usefulness of training a young daughter in the nurturant role. Neisser asks, "How much help should a girl be?" and answers:

> One mother claims the best laborsaving device known is a daughter between the ages of nine and twelve, and the danger is that you may exploit her. Direct and indirect benefits can accrue from a schoolage girl helping, in moderation, with the duties of running a house as well as with the care of younger children. A source of regret to mothers is that when their daughters are small, helping is regarded as a privilege but when the girls reach an age and attain the degree of competence when they could take over tasks, they have to be repeatedly reminded, if not coerced, to get at the dishwashing, vegetable paring, or mopping that is their lot. (p. 98)

Neisser tries to make these tasks sound intellectually challenging: "Junior housekeepers deserve to be assigned some of the creative as well as the menial jobs. The nine-year-old who dreams up a fresh, if somewhat bizarre, variation on the recurrent custard pudding is serving the cause of the family's well-being as faithfully as does the girl who scrubs the pans, and she has the reward that comes with innovation, as well." Neisser's description of the pudding as "recurrent" hints at the limitations of such ecstasies. She does not suggest that the daughter should perform such tasks because she is a member of a family in which responsibility is shared. The brother is not expected to contribute to the family's financial support, as his father does. But the daughter is not simply supposed to help with the household tasks out of duty; it is actually considered important in her development. Neisser says: "Fathers and brothers may also have domestic skills, and probably will increasingly learn to share the work of a household with the female members, but still a girl's identification with her mother is fostered through these channels." (p. 98) The perpetuation of domestic work as a female, even feminine category is thereby ensured.

The traditional role has clearly moral overtones, as noted earlier in this section. Gilligan (1978) points out the converse, how one's morality takes on the flavor of what is expected for one's sex; she suggests that men consider morality to be a question of rights, but women consider it a matter of responsibility to others. To a woman, Gilligan says, the greatest sin is to be selfish, and a woman would consider the unselfish choice to be the moral choice. She also suggests that one of the most significant influences of the women's rights movement has been to show women that they can make choices, instead of having responsibilities imposed on them, and that it is legitimate for them to consider themselves in making moral judgments.

How does the female-as-nurturer role constitute a problem for women's relationships with other women? One aspect, as noted in Chapter II, is that many factors, including society's hurry to train young females for the nurturant role, may push them early out of the nurtured role. This results in their forever feeling insecure, inadequately loved and nurtured.

When these daughters then have daughters of their own, they recognize in their small female offspring potential sources of nurturance for themselves; this combines with the mother's sense of responsibility toward society to teach daughters to nurture. One consequence is that mothers seek and come to depend upon nurturance from their daughters with an intensity that makes the girl at best uneasy and at worst nurturance-starved like her mother. Thus the cycle is perpetuated.

In a more general sense, women often grow to expect other women to be nurturant, because this fits the social expectation. For women, as for men, it is often disconcerting to encounter a woman who does not know how or does not choose to be nurturant. It is not surprising to encounter this lack of a nurturant attitude in men, but women who seek nurturance from other women and are disappointed in their expectations may experience a kind of resentment. This interacts in an interesting way with women's choice of marriage partners. Women often say they chose their husbands in part because of the men's apparent "rationality," "calm," "reasonableness." They say they felt comfortable because they knew the men would keep things under control. A slightly different approach in choosing a husband is that the woman likes to be "free to be flighty and impulsively emotional," and the husband "will bring me back down to earth—he is my hold on reality and rationality." Such women believe that because of their husbands' control of their own feelings they will be allowed to give their emotions free rein. However, as time passes, they begin to long for a man who will respond to them by showing his feelings; they learn that the control they originally found so attractive translates into emotional distance, or even contemptuous treatment, in marriage. They find that their men may place limits on how the wives can show their feelings, saying in essence: "I will let you be expressive as long as (a) it's not about me, (b) you don't expect me to show feelings in return, and (c) you will allow me to be equally salient but in the realm of control of the family power." Women may stay married to such men, maintaining a hold on a certain kind of stability, but have or dream of having lovers who will respond to them emotionally. (The male stranger at a cocktail party who immediately and deeply understands how unfeeling the woman's husband is comes to mind as the legendary figure in this situation.)

There is some historical evidence that, for the most part, women used not to expect real sharing of feelings and supportiveness from their husbands; instead, they turned to their women friends and relatives. More recently, however, greater mobility of families and breakdown of the extended family has made female friends and relatives less accessible to wives, and they are left dependent on their husbands for a close emotional relationship. This is helped, of course, if the woman is happily employed, or can stay in one place and have enough time away from home to develop real friendships with other people. But partly because of this very increase in wives' dependence on their husbands, their freedom to turn to other women is limited. For one thing, they often fear to discuss their husbands' failings with friends, feeling a duty to protect his reputation and fearing that he would be angry and even leave her helpless if he found out. So when women do turn to women friends, it is often after overcoming much reluctance. It is often, too, with the feeling that this is not their first choice, since women belong to an inferior class. When to all these feelings the assumption is added that other women are supposed to be there, ready to listen, sympathize and nurture, one's rage if they are not is understandable.

Imagine that there are two types of people in the world: one green and one red. You tell the greens, "You may not do anything except look attractive, act nice, be helpful and take care of others. Anything active, productive or pleasurable outside those limits is prohibited. In addition, if you want someone to take care of you, someone on whom you can rely, then it has to be a red. You cannot approach the red directly, nor appear to want the red to make a commitment to take care of you. You have to achieve that by being as conspicuously attractive, nice, helpful and nurturant as possible. Therefore, the main thing that can get in the way of your winning a commitment from the red is another green appearing to be more attractive, nice, helpful and nurturant than you. If a red is too rigid or limited to notice you, it is not because of any failing on red's part; nor is it because of an undesirable system that makes these rules. It is either because that other green got in the way or because you were not obviously attractive, nice, helpful and nurturant enough, or both." In this way, most of the greens' anger and fear, if not self-directed, becomes directed at other greens. Further, if greens are raised by parent greens who offer very limited love because they were similarly raised by their own parent greens, then the child greens' need to attract a red to protect them is further intensified. In this analogy, of course, the greens are in the position of most women in our society; the reds, in the traditional male position.

Dinnerstein (1977) described the double-barreled nature of woman's nurturant image: "She will be seen as naturally fit to nurture other people's individuality . . . if she fails to render them this service she is a monster, anomalous and useless." (p. 112)

In addition, the limitation of females' behavior to nurturance, frivolity and a few other categories has made it difficult for women to have confidence in their ability to form relationships or have meetings and discussions with other women that include traditionally male-identified activities. If a group of women philosophers meet and critically analyze each other's work, they are engaged in an untraditional activity for a group of females. Women often find that the newness of such endeavors causes them to feel strange and hesitant. Whereas they want something to pass among themselves that goes beyond pure nurturance and support, they may not want to subject their female peers to the same type of cutting attack that sometimes characterizes exchanges between males. In the face of such unfamiliar types of interaction among women, the temptation to retreat to female-stereotypic behavior such as nurturance—and simply to leave it at that—is strong. To give in to such temptation is to limit the possibilities for the growth of oneself and of other women.

Related to this is adopting the nurturant role as a kind of crutch: When in doubt, be nurturant. Here again, limits are placed on females' possibilities for expanding their repertoire of behavior and experience. An issue of a magazine for teenage girls in the 1960's advised: If you are nervous at a party, find someone who seems to be having a bad time and make it your business to cheer them up. One can hardly object to this advice, but one might hope that young girls would be encouraged to find other ways as well to deal with their shyness and fear in social situations.

A role frequently adopted by adolescent girls with respect to their peers is that of confidante to another girl and her boyfriend. It is more usual for girls than for boys to assume this role precisely because of females' supposed superiority in sensing and dealing with feelings. Hence one way, productive in some respects, for an adolescent girl to limit her own experience (and the risks involved) while somehow learning about heterosexual relationships is to "try to help Tom and Karen work out their problems." She can feel appropriately womanly as she hears Tom say, "I can talk to you more easily than I can talk to Karen"; she has succeeded at being nurturant, supportive, reassuring. But the jealousy that often accompanies the confidante's role, the wish to be part of such a relationship, creates resentment. The tendency is to feel like good old Aunt Bessie, the spinster, who knits mittens for her nieces and nephews because she never managed the first-choice option: marriage.

So the adolescent female confidante may continue to behave in a nurturant manner, but underneath sizzles a growing resentment of Karen, who has just what the confidante would like to have. To nurture instead of to be loved and sought after is second-rate, but she may feel it is all she can do. The insidiousness of this process is that it reinforces her sense of needing to become more feminine—like Karen—and she has learned that nurturance is a feminine thing. When she begins to sense, then, that she is not entirely pleased to be nurturant toward Tom and Karen, she quite likely decides that her dissatisfaction is a mark of insufficient womanliness and she must try harder.

One woman's resentment of another whom she believes has failed to be nurturant and responsive to her was explored earlier in this section. A specific point that warrants further discussion is the effect of the fact of death, and society's style of coping, on relationships between women.

Through the research of anthropologists and the recent writings of some psychologists, there has been increasing awareness of the relationship between reactions to death and the woman-as-nurturer role. Because it is the mother's body in which babies grow, women are often regarded as givers of life; because it is usually the mother (in North American and many other societies) who is the primary nurturer of the infant, women are often regarded as the guardians of life. Mothers come to be regarded as the source of life, fertility, creation and growth. (The reverse belief, either in historical eras or in various cultures, has often taken a form similar to Aristotle's theory: that although the woman's part may be somehow necessary, it is the man whose contribution to procreation is most important, most valued [see Lange, 1977].) But the understanding that the infant spends nine necessary months in the woman's body, and that the type of environment the mother's body provides can affect her baby's condition, easily gives rise to the labeling of women as life-givers and life-guardians. One consequence has been that women have come to seem mysterious; they have often been regarded as knowing or embodying the miracle-mystery of creation.

It would not appear a large step for either so-called "civilized" or "uncivilized" societies to expand this notion to the identification of women with the mystery and fear of death as well. The woman becomes a target, a kind of scapegoat, for the projection of the fears and angers of whole societies about death. In many societies, women are the professional or expected mourners at the time of death, and they prepare the body for burial. Such workers as Clark (1978) suggest that, from a historical perspective, men may have been energetic in seizing control of the means of production (i.e., economic power) because of some combination of their awe, fear, fascination and resentment of the woman's role in controlling the means of reproduction.

This association of women with death can be further intensified when societies hand over the lion's share of the nurturance of children to the mother (Dinnerstein, 1977). If, from infancy and childhood, one learns to turn to a single person for the meeting of one's needs, the rage at that person whenever those needs go unmet is greater than if the nurturance had been provided by more than one. (This is supported by the observation that children who live with a single parent direct more anger at that parent than if there were two parents present.) In addition, insofar as the facts of producing and protecting life imply that the giver has some power, it is a sad, hard lesson for children to learn that the mother cannot, in fact, protect them from death. This is further aggravated by the image of women as more emotional and responsive, so that they are more likely than their male mates to be asked by children for help and support in the face of fears about death. Not only can a mother not prevent her children's deaths, or the necessity of her children's confronting their own mortality, but also, since females or males can rarely think and talk about death in a comfortable way, few mothers can adequately help their children deal with their fears. The failure of support and empathy from the mother, who is expected to be a source of soothing and nurturance, makes the child angry, disappointed and resentful. This discussion applies to sons as well as daughters, of course, but the situation often becomes worse for the daughter: the son can attribute the "failure" of his mother to the general inferiority of the "other" sex, but for the daughter this would mean denigrating her own sex, with damaging consequences to her self-respect.

Devaluation of Females

The belief that males are more important and valuable than females pervades society. Women have traditionally been relieved and delighted when their first child is a boy rather than a girl. One reason is that they know their husbands would be disappointed if their first child was a girl; having had one son, neither parent need worry that they might never produce one of the highly valued sex. De Beauvoir (1974) points out:

> Investigations make it clear that the majority of parents would rather have sons than daughters. Boys are spoken to with greater seriousness and esteem, they are granted more rights; they themselves treat girls scornfully; they play by themselves, not admitting girls to their group. . . . Because of the prestige attributed to men by women, as well as the advantages they actually have, many women prefer to have sons. "How wonderful to bring a man into the world!" they say; we have seen that they dream of engendering a "hero," and the hero is obviously of the male sex. A son will be a leader of men, a soldier, a creator; he will bend the world to his will, and his mother will share his immortal fame; he will give her the houses she has not constructed, the lands she has not explored, the books she has not read. (p. 576)

A recent survey reported in *Psychology Today* (1974) showed that parents still prefer boy babies over girls. The percentage has dropped from what it was earlier in the century, however, and one reader wrote to suggest that the reduction in parents' wish for sons is due to "a breakdown in the home-and-family ideal." The reader further wrote, "The son, and in particular the eldest son is strongly tied to the archetypal family; first as its prime agent of continuation, and also as the future guardian and master of the home."

Miller and Swift (1977) discussed in some detail the greater valuation of a son compared to a daughter. They tell the story of a childless couple who adopted a baby girl rather than a boy since if the child did not live up to their expectations because of her genetic heritage, "at least she won't carry on the family." The male is seen as the carrier of the essence of the family and the race. Miller and Swift cite an article (McGrady, 1972) about sperm banking in which one donor deposited sperm even though he had male offspring of his own; he said he made the deposit in order to carry on the family line if his male offspring turned out to be sterile. Miller and Swift (1977) suggest that the sperm bank customer "believes he cannot be linked to future generations through his female offspring, should they prove fertile."

In Thomas Babe's play *A Prayer for My Daughter*, a male character describes his feelings as his wife gave birth to their child. He conveys intense excitement and happy anticipation, but when the infant turns out to be female he feels disappointed and ashamed. He fears that his having produced a daughter may indicate that he is weak, inadequate, insufficiently masculine.

A successful woman in the publishing business told the following story. She was an only child and was raised by parents who encouraged her intellectual pursuits. It never occurred to her that her parents might have preferred to have a son and would have valued him more highly than they valued her. When she was in her early twenties, she attended a party with her mother at which the topic of miscarriages arose. One woman told of a friend who had just tragically miscarried. The publisher's mother commended, "I knew a woman who had a *real* tragedy. She lost a baby through miscarriage—and it was a boy!"

The pregnant woman often feels that producing a son is a feat worthier of pride than producing a daughter. Women learn that their value lies chiefly in giving and nurturing life, and their sense of self-worth is more likely to be enhanced by giving birth to a male than to a female child. It is difficult to disregard the message emanating from the many nooks and crannies of society that males are better. Women often feel that, though insignificant themselves, they can gain recognition and a sense of substantial achievement by producing sons.

Indeed, there is impressive precedent in history and philosophy for such an attitude. Aristotle suggested the following set of explanations for the sex of an infant, based on its parents' relative contributions (Lange, 1977): If a son is born, it is because the father contributed and performed well sexually, and prevailed over the mother. If a daughter is born, it is because the mother failed, and prevailed over the father in her imperfection.

How does society's undervaluing of women interfere with women's relationships with each other? Women, like men, come to place less value on the friendship, judgment and opinions of women. When they spend time with each other, they often feel that this is only because there was no chance to spend that time with a male. Kennedy (1976) suggests that such an attitude creates what she calls "horizontal hostility":

> It's women's sense of their own lack of worth that makes sibling rivalry and horizontal hostility so easy. If you have a sense of your own worthlessness, then somebody else from your class or race or religion is clearly not to be looked up to. This is one of the bases for the pathology of women saying, "I don't get along with women. I get along with men; they're superior, so if I get along with them *I'm* superior, but I've left all my class behind." (p. 87)

The topic of aging provides an important illustration of the effect of society's undervaluing of women on their interrelationships. In North American society, as a woman ages she is usually considered to lose much of what has given her some value as a human being and a female: she has been a life-giver, but age puts an end to that; she has perhaps been beautiful (appropriate for her role as sex object or decoration), but the increase in her lines and the changes of her curve and color have typically been thought to put an end to that, too. The advertising slogan "You're not getting older; you're getting better" was effective because it filled the need for women to feel there could be something positive about their increasing age. Cosmetics and face lifts have, until very recently, been thought appropriate for women but not for men; graying hair made men distinguished but women unattractive.

Thus for women whose self-definitions were based mostly on the life-giver and/or sex-object roles, aging was often more terrifying than death. It meant they could no longer be the one or two things that were fairly certain to give them value. Appearing younger, more attractive than other women, became important. The generally held belief that women dress for other women rather than for men is one manifestation of this. Another woman's aging was a victory for oneself, like winning a race; one's own aging was a loss, making one feel inferior.

Constraints Placed on Girls

Little girls' behavior is more severely restricted than that of little boys. Greater limits are placed on girls' physical activity, sexual play and exploration, and expression of anger and aggression. These are some of the lessons society presses families to teach their children.

De Beauvoir (1974) says that the little girl

> is deprived of happy freedom, the carefree aspect of childhood . . . she is glad to become important, she talks sensibly, she gives orders, she assumes airs of superiority over her brothers of infantile rank, she converses on a footing of equality with her mother. . . . In spite of all these compensations, she does not accept without regret the fate assigned to her; as she grows, she envies the boys their vigor. . . . If the girls want to struggle with the boys and fight for their rights, they are reprimanded. They are doubly envious of the activities peculiar to the boys: first, because they have a spontaneous desire to display their power over the world, and, second, because they are in protest against the inferior status to which they are condemned. (pp. 321–22)

Perhaps the most important reason for society to suppress these kinds of behavior in girls is that they are inconsistent with the nurturant role. In most families even today, mothers do more of the child-rearing than fathers do. This means that it is usually the mother who tells the little girl not to run around so much, not to play so roughly, not to touch her genitals, not to yell so loudly, not to show her anger. And later it is the mother who tells her that her skirts are too long or too short, that she should sit with her legs carefully crossed, should not telephone boys, should not kiss a boy on the first date, should not tell a man she loves him unless he has told her first. Thus the mother becomes the carrier of the disconcerting restraints of society.

Belotti (1975), in a description of child-rearing in Italy, echoes many North American practices: "Mothers themselves recognize that they are stricter with girls . . . even more strict and demanding with daughters who are hypertonic, that is active, curious, independent, noisy, early walkers, in other words when they exhibit characteristics generally thought of as male." (p. 45) After the child's first year of life, she writes, ". . . while the mother allows or even inwardly wants her son to fight with her and get the better of her because it is in the 'natural order of things' (as it is for her to be defeated), she will not allow the girl to fight and will stamp out any of her pretensions to autonomy. She herself has been denied this autonomy and needs to take her revenge on someone, somehow." (p. 56) The following quotations from Belotti often apply not only to mothers and daughters but to any relationship between two females.

Still less does the mother tolerate competition from someone who is like herself but is not her equal. It is at this point that pitiless, direct, and thorough repression begins. Conflict itself need not appear at all with calmer, quieter girls who make less firm, less open demands for independence. On the contrary, great harmony seems to exist between mother and daughter. Apparently, they walk hand in hand, but this idyll is established and maintained wholly at the expense of the daughter. (p. 56)

These are the meek, docile girls, the mother's pets, the tame monkeys, the precocious little ladies pathologically dependent on the mother and always clinging to her. . . . In such cases open conflict does not appear even in adolescence (p. 56)

That little girls carry these restrictions into their adult lives is particularly disturbing in view of the human female's potential for thought and activity. Dinnerstein (1977) writes:

Like the male, she is equipped with a large brain, competent hands, and upright posture. She belongs to an intelligent, playful, exploratory species, inhabiting an expanding environment which it makes for itself and then adapts to. She is the only female, so far as we know, capable of thinking up and bringing about a world wider than the one she sees around her. . . . She thus seems, of all females, the one least fitted to live in a world narrower than the one around her." (p. 20)

How do the constraints on females' behavior form a barrier

between women? Women have traditionally been cast in the role of guardians of society; one is always more surprised when a girl breaks the law than when a boy does. As the keepers of society's rules, women often put puressure on each other to conform to traditional feminine roles. This is particularly the case when a female's unapproved behavior becomes public knowledge. Thus in one Midwestern high school sorority, many of whose members were sexually active, when one girl's sexual activity became explicit public knowledge that girl was "called on the carpet," subjected to pitiless verbal attack and humiliation.

Women's ostracizing of other women who "break the rules" is sometimes fueled by the fear that men who see women behaving in untraditional ways may suspect that all women have the potential to behave in such ways. As a result, men might become frightened of all women or might find the "new" types of women attractive and the traditional women uninteresting by comparison.

Fears of Homosexuality

Chapter II included an examination of how the training of girls to be nurturers can cause mothers to stop nurturing their daughters. We shall now consider society's taboo against homosexuality, which can inhibit the mother's inclinations to express her affection for her daughter.

Freud (1953, 1961, 1963) wrote that the little girl is more fortunate than the little boy because the mother-son relationship is limited by the incest taboo. A mother who had loving feelings for her son, he suggested, would have to limit her physical expression of love for him because of the risk that an incestuous encounter would ensue. While this is true, there is another strong societal norm that encourages physical displays of affection and the maintenance of some sexual tension between mother and son: the norm of heterosexuality.

If a society strongly prefers heterosexuality, it is helpful for little boys to experience early the pleasure and fascination that can come from heterosexual relationships. Their relationships with their mothers are a natural context for tantalizing, for giving little boys hints of relationships to come. This is encouraged by society's overvaluation of males compared to females, which is often reflected in the brighter sparkle in the mother's eye when she looks at her boy child. In addition, the tendency of adult males to regard adult females, including their own wives, as inferior beings, leaves many a woman longing for a close relationship with a male in which she can feel at least equal if not superior in power. The mother's relationship with her son provides just such a possibility; there she can exercise some control over a member of the highly valued male gender—control that often has sexual overtones if not overt sexual contact.

Thus we see the many factors that encourage a flirtatious, close physical relationship between mothers and their young sons. A mother moving toward her son in this way may recognize some sexual content in their relationship; but though she may react to this recognition with alarm, she can take some comfort in knowing that heterosexuality is ultimately "desirable," even if the child must find another woman to replace her as the object of those feelings. Sanger (1979) notes "the subtle deprivation of physical demonstrations of affection that little girls often suffer from their mothers which makes women more vulnerable to fear of the loss of attachment; they were never sure of it to begin with." Sanger's studies have shown that infant boys receive more direct, physical expressions of love and approval from their mothers than do infant girls.

This must be contrasted with the mother-daughter relationship. Sexual feelings between mother and daughter cannot be considered a prelude to an "acceptable" relationship later on. On the contrary, they may be a prelude to homosexuality and thus, in the eyes of most people, are to be feared. In addition, because female children are less valued than male children, their mothers are less likely to regard them as prizes whose allegiance would enhance their value by associating them with the powerful sex. In fact, even if a woman wins her daughter's admiration or interest, it is "only" the admiration of another female.

To a reader who is unfamiliar with theories of infant and child development, this emphasis on sexuality may seem curious. Therefore, I want to make it clear that mothers do not often think about these issues; rather, much of what occurs is unconscious. A sympathetic listener, however, can usually hear more intensely sexual or at least sensual content in a mother's description of her baby, and her feelings about it, than the myth of unsensual motherly love would allow. Bowlby (1978), for one, has noted how frequently mothers talk about "falling in love" with their newborns. But even if one wishes to avoid considering the sexual content in mother-infant relationships, it would be naive to assume that knowledge of a baby's sex has no effect on the mother's feelings. People who have observed a passerby on the street and then learned that the person's gender was not what they thought will readily acknowledge that gender has many subtle effects on how other people are "registered" in the observer's memory. How much more intense, then, would be the effect of a mother's original knowledge and repeated notice of her baby's gender.

With respect to the mother-daughter relationship, one important effect is the barrier placed between them by the mother's fear of raising a homosexual daughter. This barrier is so strong that to many people a mother's sensual response to her baby daughter is unthinkable. Mothers who describe the experience of nursing their sons as beautiful, even "sexy in a cute kind of way," for example, less often describe the experience of nursing their daughters in the same way. Not infrequently, they describe the latter as "strange" or "uncomfortable." This may be one of the factors contributing to the pattern Lynn (1974) noted in Mexican-American families, which seems to have more general application: the mother gives her baby daughters more attention than her sons, but after the first year the daughters are reared more severely than the sons. Belotti (1975), moreover, pointed out that women wean their daughters earlier than their sons.

That the mother-daughter relationship can include sexual wishes and feelings is clear. Consider the two following passages (Hite, 1977): "My mother and I used to hug a lot when I was young. But as I got older she sort of weaned me away from that, fearing I might turn into a lesbian." (p. 564) And from another woman: "There was a time (around age nine I'd say) when I liked to play a game with my mother: I was the princess and she was the prince. I would wear a long nightgown, and I wanted my mother to take off her dress—her stockings and garters made her look more like a prince to me. She didn't like the game at all, and would only play it reluctantly, usually not in the 'costume' I wanted." (p. 565)

Smith (1978) cites the example of Madame de Sévigné, a woman who, during the seventeenth century, wrote to her daughter:

> Love me always and forever; my existence depends on it, my soul yearns for it; as I told you the other day you are all my joy and all my sorrow. What remains of my life is over-shadowed by grief when I consider how much of it will be spent far from you.
>
> Farewell, dearest and best. Words fail me adequately to express the strength of my passion for you; they are, I find, wholly inadequate. (p. 118)

Smith notes that when this only daughter, Françoise, became the bride of a provincial nobleman and moved to the country, Madame de Sévigné launched a torrent of letters to her that flowed on, unstemmed, for a quarter of a century and included the line "Do you wonder if I cannot refrain from kissing your lovely bosom?"

Though it seems unlikely that much in the way of overtly sexual relationships occurred in the mother-daughter relationships referred to above, the intensity of many of the feelings of all three women—the fascination, even the fears of homosexuality—suggest that components of sexual feeling were present. The words of the first two women describe frequent mother-daughter situations and emotions, and even the intensity of Madame de Sévigné's feelings is striking not in kind but only in degree.

The parent who nurses a newborn is the mother. If the newborn is bottle-fed, the mother is far more likely than the father to take care of the feeding. If only one parent leaves home to work, it is more likely to be the father than the mother; thus the baby spends much more time with its female parent. If both parents go off to work, the mother is more likely than the father to rush home for lunch, leave work early and spend after-work hours with the baby, even today; moreover, the adult who stays with the baby, whether a relative, a private baby-sitter or a day-care center employee, is nearly always a woman.

Therefore, the mother—and if not she, then often another woman—is usually the person with whom the baby forms its closest relationship, and it is primarily the mother or another woman who takes care of the baby.

Freud (1932) wrote that for the baby daughter "it was really the mother who by her activities over the child's bodily hygiene inevit-

ably stimulated, and perhaps even roused for the first time, pleasurable sensations in her genitals." (p. 120) If we then come back
to our consideration of the mother's fears of producing a homosexual daughter, we reach some additional understanding. The boy's
father is likely to be at least as fearful of producing a homosexual
son as his wife is in the case of her daughter. But it is the mother
who spends the most time with the children of *both* sexes. Further,
since females are trained to be more expressive, including through
physical contact, than males, the father's relationships with his
children of both sexes are more likely to be inhibited and limited in
degree of closeness and free exchange of affection (even if only
because of his lack of practice). What this means, then, is that, if
we think of the fear of homosexuality as a door that can close
between two people, the door is less necessary, less often used in
the father-son than the mother-daughter relationship. Finding barriers and distance repeatedly imposed by the adult to whom one is
closest is at best confusing and at worst devastating to the child's
self-esteem.

The physical similarity of women (see the section below) can
lead to another source of homosexual attraction. De Beauvoir
(1974) describes what she calls the miracle of the mirror:

> When alone she does not succeed in really creating her double; if she
> caresses her own bosom, she still does not know how her breasts
> seem to a strange hand, nor how they are felt to react under a strange
> hand; a man can reveal to her the existence of her flesh *for herself—*
> that is to say, as she herself perceives it, but not what it is *to others.*
> It is only when her fingers trace the body of a woman whose fingers
> in turn trace her body that the miracle of the mirror is accomplished.
> . . . Says Colette in *Ces plaisirs:* "The close resemblance gives
> certitude of pleasure. The lover takes delight in being sure of caress-
> ing a body the secrets of which she knows, and whose preferences
> her own body indicates to her." (pp. 464–65)

What De Beauvoir and Colette are suggesting is that, even
though a woman's male lover may tell or try to show her how he
feels when she touches him or moves against him in a certain way,
she can never assume that she understands how he feels as safely
as she can assume she understands how another woman feels,
since their bodies are more nearly similar. This physical similarity
between women can be both a blessing and a curse: a curse when it

encourages the girl or woman to assume that another female understands something about her that she wishes her not to know; a
blessing when it leads to warmly shared emotional experiences,
without unpleasant intrusiveness or control. The presence of the
mother to the daughter suggests this "miracle of the mirror" and
often simultaneously frustrates it. The daughter looks at a woman
who, because of their physical similarity and the similarity of their
socialization, might well understand how she feels. If she then,
however, feels misunderstood or misused by this other female, she
is all the more upset because the promise seemed so great. Thus
many women retreat from placing this trust in other women for
fear of being deeply disappointed. Sometimes they find substitutes
by surrounding themselves with physical objects that are similar to
themselves. They learn that they are supposed to be soft and frilly,
so they acquire soft boudoirs and feathered gowns as replacements
for warm relationships with other women.

Reasons often given for women's fear of being associated with
the feminist movement are that women do not believe in bra-burn-
ing, or in being strident or aggressive, which feminists are alleged
by the media to be. But for many such women the reason is more
basic, reaching to the heart of the way society defines a "real"
woman. Being a feminist suggests that the woman's relationships
with and commitments to other women and her own independence
and self-respect may be at least as important to her as her commitment to a man.

If such women become numerous, and openly, proudly so, the
fabric of our society is endangered since distribution of economic
and political power depends on the assumption that women's first
commitment is to their husbands. Hence there has arisen the close
association, in the minds of many, between feminism and lesbianism. Both are threatening because they imply alternatives to wom-
en's role or primary devotion to the nurturing of their men. But
they are threatening for other reasons as well.

Leary (1957) has discussed the effects of emotional intensity on
interpersonal behavior. When A and B are together, if A expresses
emotions in a casual, easygoing way, B is likely to do the same. But
if A speaks intensely, B is likely to respond with the same intensity. This is partly because people usually believe that all situations
have certain rules: if one wants to be accepted into a situation, one

must learn its rules of conduct. One safe means of learning is to watch how other people behave and then to behave in similar fashion.

When we read Thoreau's statement "The majority of men lead lives of quiet desperation," we probably first respond to "desperation." But the "quiet" aspect reflects a convention of most North American societies—that even in despair, an adult is supposed to remain quiet, to keep the intensity of feelings under careful control. This is in part because many feelings are unpleasant, and when these are expressed with intensity other people have to notice something at least unpleasant and possibly painful. But many people are disconcerted even by the intense expression of love, gaiety, anticipation or hope.

Socialization is largely a process of learning which naturally occurring feelings are considered appropriate to express in which settings. Intensity and abandon compete with the power of these rules; they can have the strength of uncontrolled, even unconscious feelings. Freud (1962) suggested that individual people first formed social groups partly for protective purposes, and that in order to keep the society together these people had to suppress some of the intensity of their needs. So, for example, one person might feel some sexual desire but, instead of acting simply on that basis, would channel the energy into singing a song or gathering food for the group. The expression of feelings in an intense form, then, is a potential threat to any society since it can represent a chink in the armor that suppresses strong needs and unconscious feelings. In addition, the intense feelings of person A are a potential threat to any other person B simply because A's expression of feeling or attempt to see that A's own needs are met might interfere with B's attempts to meet B's own needs or express B's own feelings.

This brings us to one of the reasons most commonly offered for advocating male-female relationships. Males are presumably not brought up to "need" to express their feelings, but females are brought up to "need" and/or to know how to do so, depending upon which theorist is speaking. Thus male-female relationships presumably bring together some kind of ideal match: one who can and one who cannot, or need not, show strong feelings.

As males and females are now socialized, and as the myths of our society are perpetuated, most people tend to think of women as "more emotional" than men. Several things follow from this. One is that a relationship between two women would be regarded as potentially emotionally powerful. Insofar as it is true that males find it more difficult or uncomfortable to deal with strong feelings, one would expect them to feel threatened by the idea of close relationships between two women. In fact, men often find such relationships disturbing, since they seem not only potentially powerful but powerful in a way that men cannot or believe they cannot share, understand or compete with. Following on from this, men find it a particular relief to accept the societal myth that women's conversations primarily concern recipes, buttons and bows, and giggles.

Women often share these fears of emotional intensity. Women may readily admit that they married inexpressive men so that they themselves could be unrestrainedly emotional while their husbands kept in touch with the practical, rational realities of life "for" them. Just as children are best able to laugh and cry without inhibition when they know their parents will protect them from external threats, so women have often chosen their husbands to serve such a function for them. Thus the stereotype of "woman as child" is given a basis in reality. Women who marry "good, solid, unemotional" men and then go through life freely indulging momentary impulses, demanding that their intense needs be repeatedly met, become unable to act otherwise. In an adult, such behavior is appropriately called childish, selfish and irresponsible.

An additional consequence of classifying women as the emotionally intense sex is women's fears of forming close relationships with each other. Insofar as their emotional unrestrainedness has been permitted by their husbands, women often find that such behavior has different effects in the presence of another woman. This gives rise to the competitive, jealous, childish behavior often observed between two what are commonly called very "feminine" women. Even for adult, responsible women who are not self-indulgent, there is real cause to fear that being around another woman will arouse feelings and fears with a degree of intensity that is less likely to occur in the presence of a man. Returning for a moment to Leary's work, we recall that intensity of feeling in one person tends to elicit similar intensity in the other. Two women are more likely to have been encouraged to express many emotions freely than have two men, or one woman and one man. It is thus realistic for one woman to fear that in the presence of another woman she herself will experience the full intensity of her own feelings and find it hard to suppress them.

One specific, important aspect of feelings between women concerns the female friends and relatives of women who are actively homosexual. If one woman knows that her female friend is actively heterosexual, she can assume that the friend's association with males involves some control of expression of feeling. But if she knows that her friend's closest, even sexual relationships are with other women, she may assume that her friend is in closer touch with her feelings than is a heterosexual woman. Thus many mothers, sisters, friends of women who become actively homosexual report that, after discovering the sexuality of the other woman, they are suddenly reluctant to greet them with hugs or to talk openly. Such a reaction goes well beyond the fear that the homosexual woman might try to seduce them. It is a fear of encountering their own strongest feelings, wishes and fears. This is also one reason many people find it somehow more comforting to think that, even within a lesbian relationship, one partner behaves as a traditional male and one as a traditional female: in such a case, perhaps the degree to which the participants' feelings are expressed intensely, and the degree to which they are in touch with material that most people keep unconscious, is assumed to be smaller.

The Mother's Similarity to the Daughter

Another source of hostility between women is their similarity. This includes their physical likenesses, of course, but it also includes the fact that society classifies them both as "females" and then treats them similarly in many respects. An extension of the latter is that daughters know that mothers are in some ways grown-up daughters: "That's me in thirty years."

There are several consequences of this similarity, some of which have been mentioned in previous sections. One is that the mother not only sets limits on her daughter's behavior but also exemplifies the limits of socially acceptable female roles. Our society being what it is, these limits have often been narrow. So when a daughter looks at her mother and thinks, "That's me in thirty years," she also realizes that her mother is the prime factor in shaping her. Therefore, the mother who has kept her own behavior and aspirations within the narrow limits of what society allows to women is a living example of the poverty of possibility that she leaves open for her daughter's future.

Of the mothers who have accepted the traditional female roles in our society, some seem contented but others clearly are not. Of those who are not, some will tell you so point-blank, others are aware of some uneasiness or dissatisfaction, and still others repress all awareness of their discontent; the last group may develop physical symptoms, depressions, anxiety attacks or "bitchy" styles of behavior. We know that children are unusually sensitive to their parents' dissatisfactions. Thus, when a mother is dissatisfied with her own traditional female role but is raising her daughter to fit that role, the daughter will probably in some way feel the effects of such ambivalence. She may not learn to accept the traditional role wholeheartedly, in which case both she and her mother will feel that her mother's endeavors have failed. Or she may resent her mother for giving her two contradictory messages: "Do X and you will be happy," and "I am doing X and I am unhappy." This point will be discussed further in the following chapter, as it becomes especially important during the daughter's adolescence and young adulthood.

There is a further effect of the mother-daughter similarity. We know from developmental psychology that children often believe parents can read their thoughts. In fact, they may do so with good reason, because parents who spend much time with their children and who are sensitive to them are likely to some degree to sense what the children feel. But this early belief dies a slow death, particularly in cases where parents are sensitive to their children's needs. (And parents differ in the extent to which they use this sensitivity for the child's good or as an instrument of power and intrusion.)

When we add to this the consideration that people generally assume they are most easily understood by people who are most similar to themselves, we find another potential source of daughter-mother hostility. The daughter who wishes for privacy of thought and action may come to believe that her mother nevertheless knows what she thinks, what she wishes, what she feels.

The situation is exacerbated by the fact that the mother is usually the parent who spends the most time with the children. So, every time the daughter turns around, she faces a kind of mirror, her mother. She has a thought, a fear, a wish, and she sees her mother watching her. Especially as she grows older and realizes that her mother was once her age, she wonders (or fears) whether her mother knows what she feels; the mother often knows facts about her daughter's situation: e.g., it's prom night and she has no date, or her first period has just begun, or she likes to climb the playground rope because it feels good. This makes the issues of separation and individuation of the daughter from the mother particularly difficult. Since these issues are paramount in adolescence, they will be discussed in more detail in the appropriate section of the following chapter. But they can have far-ranging effects much earlier as well and must be kept in mind in considering the developmental course of the daughter-mother relationship.

Because of physical similarity and the similarity of their social roles, women often regard each other as the ultimate judges of their success, the mirrors of their reality. It is often said that women take pains with their appearance because of a concern more for other women's opinions than for those of men. At a different level, a woman who uses the so-called feminine techniques of flirtation, manipulation and game-playing to attract men tends to believe that other women can see through such techniques; hence she may regard other women as potential threats to her image. Similarly, if she can dress or attract a man in a way that inspires the envy of other women, she may feel that she has passed the most important test. The person who one believes can sit in judgment easily becomes feared and resented, so women fear and resent each other.

Even today, within numerous fields women account for very small proportions of the work force. This constitutes a further source of hostility and conflict. A given man in a field made up mostly of men will be described differently from the rare woman in that field. A male philosopher, for example, may become known as "the philosopher at the University of Smithville who specializes in Aristotle"; a male assembly-line worker, as "the man who can put the finishing touches on the Chevy chassis faster than any other man in the plant." But a woman in the philosophy department is more likely to become known as "the woman philosopher at the University of Smithsville" (or worse still, the blonde); a woman at the plant, as "our first woman chassis completer." When a second woman enters either situation, she destroys the first woman's uniqueness and accustomed label: the first women is no longer "our woman here." Then both women have to try to make their reputations on the basis of their specific work. The men have been doing this all along, but it is more difficult for the women because there are still only two, and thus the eye of the office is more critically on them as they attempt to prove that management or administration was justified in hiring them. Women trained to win approval and acceptance by being "feminine" find the label *"the woman here in our office"* accustomed, easy, compared to the need to prove themselves. Even women who take their job seriously and want to prove the worth of their work per se naturally resent the loss of the quick-and-easy label. This is not to ignore, of course, the other side of the coin—that being the only woman places a greater burden on one to prove oneself; both kinds of feelings often coexist, in varying proportions.

CHAPTER 4

Daughter-Mother Conflict

This chapter traces some sources of barriers between daughters and mothers, beginning before the daughter is born and continuing through her adulthood. Though many conflicts emerge in varying forms at more than one stage, they will be mentioned primarily at the stage at which they seem paramount.

In considering the sources of daughter-mother difficulties, it is important to keep in mind a point made earlier—that conflict per se is not harmful. But it must also be remembered that conflict for girls and women is aggravated by the fact that aggression, competition and anger are branded as unfeminine.

When aggression and anger pass between males, they know that such expression is permitted, even encouraged, as part of the masculine role. The same is true for competitive feelings and behavior. Therefore, the tensions that arise in the course of males' relationships have sex-appropriate outlets. Some obvious examples are competitive sports and hunting: the former allow males to direct these feelings toward each other, the latter to displace them onto animals. Even vigorous physical activity like running or mountain climbing, which has either no clear object or an inanimate one and yet allows release of tension, has often been branded unfeminine; this is a leftover from Victorian standards but is a potent controller of behavior.

What, then, happens to girls' needs to achieve and compete? These needs do not disappear but rather become restricted, through socialization, to the safely female sphere. High school girls form "clubs" in which members compete to see who, for example, can "get" the most boys to like her. Males' talk of achievement and competition often sounds tough and frightening, especially if it concerns contact sports or corporations that control people's lives and money. But within females' restricted sphere special forms of language and facial expressions are learned that allow them to use nearby individuals (family, husband, children) and their achievements as emblems and expressions of the females' own suppressed behavior and feelings. Women then may discuss trivialities or very personal things—the age at which the baby speaks a first word, or a recipe for carrot cake—with an intensity that does not befit them and can make them seem, by contrast, ridiculous.

Children of both sexes often learn to devalue the mother because she is female, and children of both sexes direct anger at her as a way to become independent of the primary attachment. While boys are devaluing their mothers, they can be emulating their fathers as standards of conduct. But the very mothers whom girls devalue are the people whose behavior they are encouraged to emulate.

These themes pervade many stages of the daughter-mother relationship and can serve as a background for the discussion of development that follows.

Before the Child Is Born

Society's preference for male children has been discussed in Chapter III, but further detail is appropriate here. De Beauvoir (1974) describes, in a number of societies and historical eras, the tendency of mothers to reject female infants and take pride in male infants. When infanticide, the killing of babies, has been practiced on just one sex, the typical pattern has been that girl babies were killed because they were not as highly valued as boy babies. In his book about child abuse, for example, Smith (1975) points out that "as late as 1873 female infanticide was permitted in China" (pp. 3–5) and that certain groups of Arabs used to kill their daughters. When girl babies have been saved, it has usually been because they were needed as helpers or slaves.

Even today, no one is surprised to hear a parent boast of a newborn son: "He'll grow up to be President," but if the same boast is made of a newborn daughter, no one is quite certain whether or not it was meant as a joke. It is not unusual for a parent to say with tear-filled eyes, "I hope I live to see my son graduate from college," but the analogue (which is not really analogous) for the daughter is "I hope to live to dance at her wedding." For the son, college is to be the beginning of achievements, but for the daughter the wedding is the peak of achievement (except, of course, for motherhood).

Another factor that affects the parent's wishes concerning the sex of their unborn child is the carrying on of the family (usually the husband's) name. Most children are given the last name of their father. The boy, when grown, may produce children who will in turn pass on the name of their father and paternal grandfather. But the daughter will probably give her children (whether male or female) the last name of her husband. The best hope for the wife, who at marriage sacrifices her family's (i.e., her father's) name, is to please her husband by giving him sons who will carry on his name.

Infant and Mother

When my first child was born and I tried to describe my joy to a child psychologist friend who had no children, she said, "Yes, I know. Babies are so helpless that you really feel they need you." At that point, my baby was several days old. I was familiar with the theory that nature makes sure its babies are well cared for by preprogramming mothers to respond to their helpless behavior. But in the presence of my baby I had not stopped to recall any theories. I found myself too absorbed by the wealth of emotions stirred up in me during those early days. Thus, when my friend referred to the helplessness theory and my instant reaction was puzzlement, I began to consider the nature of my reactions to my baby.

What I noticed, and what other mothers have since corroborated, is that, though the baby's frequent needs for help do tend to elicit the mother's tendency to give that help, another factor is at least as important in the forming of a close relationship between mother and child. (This close relationship is sometimes called "bonding" and can apply equally to the development of close relationships between infants and their fathers, or indeed between infants and any adult who spends a lot of time in close contact with them.) This other factor is the infant's lack of emotional defensiveness. Defenses are sometimes defined (Sullivan, 1953) as strategies that people develop in order to cope with anxieties. For example, as an infant grows into childhood, when needs for security and tenderness are not met the defense of denial might develop; in this case, the child would tend to push these needs, or at least the feeling that they were not met, out of consciousness and, if asked, would deny having such needs. Or the child may develop the defense of projection, in which one attributes one's own needs and traits to others. Thus a child whose need for affection and nurturance is not met might assume that most people are very lonely. Whether or not there is truth in this belief, it provides a means of coping, of defense against the pain of one's own needs not being met.

Without defenses, our feelings appear in all their raw intensity. In the adult-infant relationship, this intensity becomes meaningful for two reasons. One is that an adult rarely encounters another person who has so few defenses; most adults and children have complicated, sophisticated systems of defense. The other reason is that, as Leary (1957) has explained, the intensity of one person's expression of feeling is a major determinant of the intensity of the other person's emotional response.

Therefore, the fullness of the infant's rage, the totality of the infant's delight, the extreme despair of the infant's response to separation from the close parent—all tend to elicit intense feelings from the parent and can be responsible for the development of an intense parent-infant relationship. While such a relationship helps in the "bonding" process, it also gives rise to many feelings that are often left out of myths about motherhood. Motherhood is supposed to be serene, but mothering an infant actually produces some of the most intense feelings of panic, fear, rage and despair that adults can experience. These occur because the infant's needs seem unmeetable, the infant's messages expressed in wails are unclear, the infant needs things just when the parents are exhausted or about to make love, or the parent is preparing to leave the infant for the first time.

This intensity adds force to other aspects of mother-child interactions. So, for example, the mother's admiration of her sons can often more appropriately be called adoration. Her flirtatious and seductive behavior toward him may become overheated and may even stop just short of incest. Her need to be needed by him is played out in an intensification of her nurturant role to an extreme degree, as in the cases of mothers who brag that their sons "never lifted a finger" to help in the house, or that they cleaned out the bathtub after the son bathed until he left home at the age of thirty-five.

Why would the typical mother-infant relationship be more intense than the typical father-infant relationship? First of all, since males are taught to inhibit their expressions of warmth and tenderness, by the time they become fathers they are less likely than women to allow themselves to be fully drawn into intense relationships with their infants. Indeed, if they did act on the full intensity of the feelings their babies elicit, they would spend less time and energy on their vocations, thus failing to conform to the stereotypic male image. Females, to the contrary, are trained to act on the full intensity of loving, tender feelings their babies elicit.

Mothers who also work outside their own homes are more likely than working men at least to feel that, when home, they not only may but also *should* interact intensely with their infants. Therefore, even if they have an outside job, their intimate relationships with their infants can serve to help them carry out the stereotypic female role.

It is against this background of an intense mother-infant relationship that a girl baby experiences an interruption, a decrease more rapid than what her brother experiences, as the mother begins to prepare her daughter for the nurturant role.

A sudden failure in the meeting of a previously met need can cause one to experience that need as more intense than before (Freud, 1905). If, during the period of earliest infancy, a daughter has an intensely loving relationship with her mother and then is subjected to strict limitations on the expression of that loving intensity, she could well begin to experience herself as a person whose need for love is never met. Such a period of deprivation, begun early in life and following after a period of feeling well loved, can leave females with a sense of loss that can never be overcome.

A woman can never again be an infant or a young child; she cannot return to her prior levels of cognitive, emotional and physical development. So, even if she manages to establish a close, loving relationship with someone, the experience of that love cannot have as great an effect her as when she first experienced a loss of love and nurturance.

Insofar as the mother enjoys an intense relationship with her infant daughter, she may be reluctant to alter that relationship in any way for fear that some intensity and closeness will be lost. But as the infant grows, the mother's fears about homosexuality (see Chapter III) may be aroused, in proportion to the intensity of her loving feelings for her daughter. In such cases, the more intense the early relationship, the stronger will be the limits that the mother feels she must impose on her interactions with her daughter.

The fear of homosexuality has at least two aspects: the mother may fear that she will produce a homosexual daughter, and she may also fear, if she feels a strong emotional or physical response toward her infant daughter, that she is herself homosexual. Belotti (1975) has pointed out in this connection that mothers prefer to breast-feed boys rather than girls. This may be due to a combination of fears of homosexuality and the pushing of the daughter into the nurturant role (see Chapter III). Both clinically and in informal exchanges, however, women often acknowledge feelings of comfort, even of physical pleasure, while nursing their infant sons but some discomfort while nursing their infant daughters—despite the fact that infant girls are usually considered calmer and easier to care for than infant boys.

The point in a daughter's development at which the mother begins to distance herself in order to guard against homosexuality varies a great deal. One determining factor is how wide a range of behavior the mother considers to be sexual. A rigid mother who feels that any sign of sensuality is dangerously sexual is likely to put physical and emotional distance between herself and her daughter early in the child's life. A mother who is comfortable with physical expressions of affection and who has confidence in her own ability to set limits, to draw the line when she feels expressions become too nearly sexual, will be likely to set those limits later in the child's life and to set them less stringently. Some mothers will consider any physical contact with even their infant daughters sexually threatening, whereas others will happily go through life hugging, kissing and caressing their daughters without fearfully interpreting this as homosexual behavior. In some cases, an individual other than the mother may cause the distancing process to begin. A father who observes his wife to be more relaxed in her physical expressions of love with her daughter than she is with him may feel that his own sexuality is threatened and may try to put a stop to this type of mother-daughter interaction.

Regardless of who initiates the distancing, the daughter usually sees the mother as being responsible. Not understanding societal prohibitions of homosexuality and their relationship to her mother's changed behavior, the daughter may experience feelings of rejection. Children's typical response to rejection is to look within themselves for the reason. They wonder, "What did I do to make her love me less?"

A somewhat similar situation occurs in mother-son relationships, though it is the prohibition of incest, rather than homosexuality, that operates here. But mothers and sons have a well-established alternative. They may withdraw physically from each other in some ways, but they may flirt outrageously. A mother's coy, seductive behavior toward her son is countenanced by society as appropriate encouragement of the son's heterosexuality and acknowledgment of male superiority. This teaches the young male child that he is a privileged person, a male. Society does not offer such support where daughters are concerned. Some father-daughter flirtation is countenanced, of course, but there is a difference. The father was not the daughter's primary love object. Moreover, being male, it is unlikely that he would be as warm and expressive as his wife, so there would be limits on his behavior even if he had been the girl's primary love object.

Neither sons nor daughters easily forget the love and nurturance they receive from their mothers during infancy. Therefore, the daughter whose mother begins to distance herself has the added frustration of recalling the way the mother used to treat her. This gives rise to a more complex feeling in children who have been well loved and nurtured than in children who have had no such experience. In some sense, every time the daughter looks at her now more distant mother, she feels a pull toward the past in which she felt more protected and loved. The very presence of her mother is a seductive reminder both of present rejection and distance and of past protection and love.

Another source of rejection that affects the baby daughter is her parents' disappointment that she is not a boy (see Chapter III).

Without understanding their source, she can sense the anxiety, rejection and even dislike that this disappointment produces. As she grows older, she may become aware of the reasons for her sadness and the extent to which they have their roots in her gender. But the seeds of her lack of self-esteem and her anger are sown with awesome firmness in the first years of her life, when she experiences herself as one who does not give pleasure and who is not cherished. This is all the more worrisome because of the totality of infants' and young children's experience. Most of their emotional life occurs within the parent-child relationship. It might almost be said that, for infants, the world *is* how their parents feel and make them feel. One only rarely experiences such totality, such a surround of feeling, after infancy. It can occur in dreams, or at certain times in psychoanalysis, when a sadness or an ecstasy is felt with an inexpressible fullness and absorption: one almost seems to *be* the feeling. Much of infants' experience is probably like this, and so we begin to understand the depth and intractability of the insecurity and poor self-regard of women and girls whose parents wished they were boys.

In Chapter III, some problematic consequences of the mother's and daughter's similarities of body and gender were noted. Even in the daughter's infancy, the fact that the daughter is female, like herself, may precipitate a reexperiencing in the mother of her own unmet needs. When she recognizes her daughter's feelings and needs, she may feel a reawakening of her own feelings in a way that is hard to control. She may wish that someone would give her some nurturance that is as reassuring as the nurturance she wants to offer her daughter. It is at this time that there comes into play the mother's understanding that society wants her to raise her daughter to become a nurturer. This makes it easy for the mother to turn to her daughter, in the hope that the daughter will love and take care of her (see Chapter II). (Chesler, 1973, alludes to, but unfortunately does not fully examine, the pattern of an insufficiently nurtured mother being unable to nurture her daughter adequately, and the daughter thereby nurturing her own daughter deficiently.) With society's encouragement, the very intensity of the mother's relationship with her infant, and her awareness of the strength of the infant's feelings and needs, may make it difficult for her to set limits on her own needs and wishes for nurturance.

Society dictates that a good mother train her daughter to be a nurturer; what better place to begin, therefore, than in teaching her to take care of her closest companion, her mother? The mother who might otherwise feel too guilty about asking her daughter to meet her needs is "helped" by the knowledge that, in the eyes of society, she is "doing the right thing." If the daughter practices well the care and protection of her mother, then she will be well prepared to become society's ideal: a woman who can nurture her husband and sons. If she begins to regard such behavior as an obligation in infancy or early childhood, then so much the better for society, since she will feel that it "comes naturally." She will believe that this is what she is supposed to do, and she may even feel uncomfortable or unnatural behaving otherwise.

Child and Mother

Readers who are interested in theoretical issues may wish at this point to refer back to the section on the cognitive-developmental approach in Chapter I. Around the toddler stage, as described in that theory, with the acquisition of language children soon begin to understand differences of gender: Mommy is a girl, and I am a girl, and my brother is a boy, and Daddy is a boy, right? Then, much as a child wishes to avoid behaving like a younger child (hence the usefulness of the "only babies throw their food" type of statement in shaping behavior), so most children wish to increase their repertoire of behavior appropriate to their gender. Erikson (1959) has pointed out that, though the identity *crisis* typically occurs in adolescence, even young children begin to learn, expand and check up on their identity in a process that is really lifelong. Children's need for competence (White, 1959) probably provides at least some of the motivation, in addition to the human need to decrease uncertainty. Thus the child who has learned that she is a girl begins with great energy to seek information: What do girls do? I'll do that. Is that right? Goody!

That identification and a serious attitude toward developing and understanding one's identity begin very early is reflected in the behavior of a child as early as the second year of life. Put a new hat or an apron on a two-year-old, and the child is not likely to laugh (as observing adults or other children might do); rather, the child typically adopts a solemn air as though aware that something of great importance is taking place. Often the child goes to a mirror to inspect the new image, perhaps in an attempt to find out what the new element does as far as identity is concerned: When I wear this, how do I look? Who am I now, and how does such a person behave? It is all the more impressive when the new element promotes the recognition of one's gender. The importance of the discovery of one's gender is increased partly by the knowledge that it is the same as that of one of the parents. And the mirror in the case of a child's gender is how the parents and the rest of society seem to feel about this new "hat," this new "girl" or "boy" label: I will feel proud to belong to this gender if the people around me seem to feel that my gender warrants pride.

It is during the toddler stage that children turn categories and labels over and over in their minds, testing when they are appropriate and how far they can be pushed. In preschool, if encouraged to do something they are reluctant to do, they refuse on such grounds as "Girls don't ever climb ladders."

Whom do young children look to as the authority on such categories? Usually, first and foremost, the mother. For the daughter, the mother is the resource person: What is a girl supposed to do, Mommy? The mother is the instrument that executes society's "will." Through their own socialization experiences, mothers have learned what society considers appropriate for girls, and most mothers feel it is their duty to teach their daughters these rules. By this process, then, the mothers of daughters in the toddler stage and then later childhood are usually involved in executing society's prescriptions: teaching their daughters to suppress certain types of feelings, or at least to refrain from showing them, limiting them to "feminine" behavior.

Griffin (1977, p. 101) describes mother and daughter trapped in women's traditional passive and domestic roles:

At home
my daughter waits,
the innocent jailer

together
we grow pale

doing dishes
and answering the telephone.

De Beauvoir (1974) says that while it is most often the mother who imposes the socially dictated restrictions on the daughter's behavior (at least until the girl reaches adolescence or becomes potentially or actually sexually active), it is often the father who encourages more assertive, less restricted behavior:

> She is treated like a live doll and is refused liberty. Thus a vicious circle is formed; for the less she exercises her freedom to understand, to grasp and discover the world about her, the less resources will she find within herself, the less will she dare to affirm herself as subject. If she were encouraged in it, she could display the same lively exuberance, the same curiosity, the same initiative, the same hardihood, as a boy. This does happen occasionally, when the girl is given a boyish bringing up; in this case she is spared many problems. It is noteworthy that this is the kind of education a father prefers to give his daughter; and women brought up under male guidance very largely escape the defects of femininity. (p. 316)

De Beauvoir's comments are consistent with the research on the achievement-oriented behavior of women, which apparently depends more on whether their fathers encouraged them to achieve than on whether their mothers did. (This pattern may be in part a consequence of the devaluation of women: If mother encourages me to achieve, who is she, anyway? But if father encourages it, I want to please him.) As long as the responsibility for child-rearing is disproportionately left to women, daughters will experience their mothers as the sources of limitations that are arbitrary and oppressive.

The mother's imposition of these severe restraints on her daughter's freedom is in some sense tantamount to a lessening of nurturance. She must reduce the daughter's exuberance, assertiveness and aggressiveness. In effect, she gives the daughter the message: "This aspect of you is not good, and therefore I do not accept, love or cherish it. I love and nurture only what will disconcert neither me nor someone else." What usually strengthens these nonverbal or, more rarely, verbal messages is the mother's own early experience of rejection when she herself behaved "inappropriately." This adds a kind of emotional shudder and dread to the mother's demeanor as she attempts to teach her daughter to live within the prescriptions of society, and the daughter thus senses that breaking such rules would precipitate some special horror, perhaps both for her and for her mother.

Rich (1976) writes: "And it is the mother through whom patriarchy early teaches the small female her proper expectations. The anxious pressure of one female on another to conform to a degrading and dispiriting role can hardly be termed 'mothering,' even if she does this believing it will help her daughter to survive." (p. 243)

Below are two illustrations of how families can produce what is known as a "difference-amplifying effect" with respect to casting daughters in the nurturant role. One family included a father, a mother who was committed to a time-consuming vocation, twins named Jane and John, and four younger children. Although Jane and John were almost exactly the same age, because Jane was the girl she was given the responsibility for much of the raising of the other children. Once she had been cast in this role as a young child and rewarded for carrying out a bit of it, she discovered she had a sure-fire way of gaining praise and acceptance, and her family increasingly thought of her as "the little mother." In this manner, her caretaking behavior came to consume progressively more of her time and energy, while John continued to be allowed to be a child.

The second family consisted of the parents, twin daughters named Eleanor and Emily, and two younger children. Eleanor was a few minutes older than Emily, but she and the rest of the family quite seriously referred to her as "the oldest." From the time she was a toddler, she was given many more housekeeping and child-care duties than Emily. When the twins were seen at age fifteen, Eleanor dressed and acted in many ways that made her appear strikingly more mature than Emily, and they both clearly felt that Eleanor had more responsibility for holding their troubled family together than Emily.

One tragic extreme of the consequences of mother using daughter to meet the family's needs and being unable to support the daughter occurs in the case of father-daughter incest (Gadlin, 1978; Kaplan, 1978). This type of incest is only beginning to be publicly noted, and preventive action at the level of social policy is in its infancy. It is much more common than was previously believed. Gadlin (1978) points out that incest does not often occur in glaringly abnormal families but rather is found in families where society's usual patterns are merely somewhat intensified; that is, the father has the power in the household, and the mother and other females attempt to meet his demands. Totah (1979) observes that in such families one frequently finds a mother-daughter role reversal, with the mother inadequately nurturing and inadequately allying herself with the daughter. Totah believes that this is usually because of some severe emotional deprivation in the mother's own early childhood. In her role as nurturer, then, the daughter does not often receive flattering or affectionate kinds of attention. Encouraged by the social view that men's attention is more valuable than women's, and further by the fact that her father's presence at home is more unusual than her mother's, the daughter may come to feel that even her father's sexual demands on her are a type of attention worth having.

It has been asserted, mostly by male mental health workers, that the mothers in these families are often sexually frigid or uninterested, and that they consciously or unconsciously encourage the incest between the husband and the daughter in essence to "keep him off my back." But Totah has found that mothers often seem unaware of the incest primarily because they are so insecure and have such intense fears of loss and separation that they will not risk a confrontation: they fear losing both husband and daughter. This characterizes their way of dealing not only with incest but also with nearly everything in their families: the husband's word is law, every one of his demands, no matter how unreasonable, must be met. In such families, says Totah (1979), both husband and wife are often very emotionally needy people who had little nurturance in their own childhood. However, the different patterns of socialization for men and for women lead them into the "acceptable" marital pattern: the man rules the house with unreasonable demands in an attempt to have his own immense needs met, and the mother and children try desperately to meet his needs for fear that otherwise he will leave them.

Media personnel contacted a colleague of mine and asked him whether he did not think that father-daughter incest was an exquisitely beautiful thing, since it combined both the closeness of a sexual relationship and the gentle love of a father-daughter relationship. What must be understood is that even the extra attention and sexual arousal the daughter may experience usually have harmful consequences. Often, a pattern is set so that in times of loneliness or stress as an adult the incest victim attempts to cope by seizing on a father-figure and becoming impulsively sexually involved or even pregnant, rather than learning to be self-reliant or to turn to female friends and relatives or even males in a nonsexual relationship. Because it is probable that her mother managed to ignore the incest for a long time or even to defend her husband against the daughter's eventual accusations, the daughter learns to mistrust other women deeply.

In the more frequent, milder cases where incest does not occur but females are devalued and the mother does not offer her daughter much support or regard for her worth as a female, the daughter also tends to turn to men as though they were the solution to all her problems. This situation can be fostered even in families with adequate mothers. Dinnerstein (1977) demonstrates that the mother is the primary child-raiser in most families, that it is she who imposes most of the routine discipline, and these factors combine with society's undervaluing of females to render the father's attention still more special and desirable. This carries over extensively into adulthood, so that women often feel that relationships with other women give them less prestige and generally have less to offer than do relationships with men.

During the toddler and childhood years, a phenomenon that was discussed in Chapter III becomes important. That is the child's belief that her mother can read her thoughts. It is a human tendency to assume that people who are similar to ourselves have feelings that are similar to ours. The assumption is strikingly prevalent for gender groups: in North American society, females tend to assume that other females share their feelings and motives, and the same is true for males and other males.

It is almost a defining feature of childhood that children believe parents know what goes on in their minds. This belief usually weakens as the child grows older, but remnants of it often persist even into adulthood. In addition, parents have a great deal of legal and emotional power over their children, and another human inclination is to assume that those who hold power also have special knowledge. (Consider, for example, how many Americans defended President Johnson's decision to bomb North Vietnam on the grounds: "He's the President; he must have special knowledge, unavailable to us, that justified that decision.") Such beliefs can be comforting to a daughter, in the context of a warm parent-child relationship, when she feels frightened or insecure. But when the daughter is angry, especially at her mother, when she feels any "bad" feelings or has "evil" thoughts (e.g., "I want to hurt my baby brother," or "I want to steal that toy from the store"), her belief in her mother's extraordinary powers can become a curse. She fears retribution for these feelings or thoughts, and she imagines her mother as the instrument of retribution. When she is exploring the world around her, developing a sense of competence and a sense of the effect her actions have on other people, the belief that her mother can read her thoughts can have disturbing consequences. It can confuse the child about her own reasons for doing things. The following account is one that I have heard, in forms that vary only slightly, from many women, both in psychotherapy and in various social and academic contexts.

From as far back as she could remember, Elizabeth believed that it was important to be "good," considerate of other people's feelings and anxious to help and to please. Though as a young girl she began to realize that she was intelligent and talented, she still felt that the most valuable part of her was that "good," helpful core: all her life her mother had said things like "That nice old Mrs. Taylor says you always stop and talk so sweetly to her—you just never forget." When Elizabeth first recalled these comments as an adult, they appeared to have been very frequent. But what later became clear was that they may not actually have been particularly frequent but had tremendous impact on her, because she had been taught that the best thing a girl could possibly do was to "be sweet." So these comments were a kind of yardstick by which she could measure the degree of success she was having in trying to be sweet. The potentially insidious nature of such comments becomes clear, however, when we listen further to the story. As the child grew, and as she realized how important it was to have other people consider her helpful and sweet, she began to doubt that she truly had those qualities "deep down inside." She wondered whether it wasn't all an act, performed out of fear of her mother's disapproval or out of the overwhelming need for her mother's approval. When her mother asked her to "be a sweetie, and set the table," she never felt sure whether she would have been "good" enough to offer to set the table if her mother had not asked.

Now, one would not want mothers to stop praising their daughters for doing things that help other people. Praise can be an effective way to encourage sharing and kindness in our children. But potential for destruction comes from the fact that females' roles are so restricted. The growing male may or may not be kind, but he knows that his value to society can lie acceptably in his career. For the growing female, being the caretaker has for so long been the primary route to acceptability and security that an unwarranted amount of energy goes into trying to achieve that role and wondering whether she is "really" warm and kind. Her fear is that, if she is not, she can never let up, never relax her vigilance, or the evil, the "selfishness" inside her, will break through and she will be disgraced, revealed as having needs of her own and impure thoughts.

Adolescent and Mother

Increase in Sexuality and Aggression

In normal adolescence, as part of the developmental processes around puberty, girls and boys experience an increase in both sexual and aggressive feelings based largely on biological changes. The degree to which adolescents are frightened, pleased or indifferent about these changes of feeling, and about the changes that occur in various parts of their bodies, varies widely. Many of the physical changes can be observed by other people—if not in public, then at least in locker rooms. By avoiding these situations, or taking great care, adolescents can conceal some of these changes; others, however, such as growth of the girl's breasts or the increase in the boy's facial hair or changing voice, are harder to conceal.* The latter have clearly occurred and apparently not be-

_____

*De Beauvoir (1974) describes the young adolescent girl's feeling that her "body is getting away from her, it is no longer the straightforward expression of

cause of the child's wishes or fears, and the difficulty of conceal-
ment puts some pressure on the adolescent to come to terms with
these changes, by accepting, denying or feeling angry about them.

Changes in sexual and aggressive feelings are still more complex
in their effects on the adolescent. First of all, it is very easy, when
one notices a change in one's feelings, to search for some cause for
that change. People are more comfortable when they can explain
things than when they have to live with uncertainty; this is especially true with respect to feelings. It is not pleasant to feel that
one's emotions are subject to arbitrary and inexplicable change.
Few adolescents are informed of the emotional changes or increases in sexual and aggressive drives that occur at that stage in
life. Yet even for those who are informed, foreknowledge often
does little to help in coping with the changes.

There are three reasons for this. One is that, even when fore-
warned, an adolescent who experiences a new or more intense
feeling may not recognize its nature. A woman in her late twenties
told me what first attracted her, in her very early teens, to the man
she later married. "He drove a neat car, he was polite, and there
was something I felt whenever he was around. I didn't know what
it was at the time, but I later realized that he was very sexy." Greer
(1970) describes the process by which sexual feelings and the female's need for security are intensely romanticized, to the point
where young girls expect that the world will change the first time a
boy kisses them. These layers of romanticism combine with the
confusing messages girls receive about whether or not they are
supposed to be sexy (often resolved in North America by the female who uses baby powder and baby shampoo, looks wide-eyed
and innocent, is very sexy but apparently unaware that she is).
Therefore, the adolescent girl often encounters considerable
blocks if she tries to identify her changing feelings.

The second obstacle to adolescent girls' understanding of phy-
siologically based changes is the human tendency to attribute feelings to changes in situation rather than to hormonal changes.
Women may be aware that they feel depressed just before their

---

her individuality; it becomes foreign to her; and at the same time she becomes for
others a thing; on the street men follow her with their eyes and comment on her
anatomy. She would like to be invisible; it frightens her to become flesh and to
show her flesh." (p. 346)

menstrual period begins, but they may nevertheless routinely attribute the depression to recent life events. For a woman who has
just given birth or weaned a nursing baby, no amount of understanding that hormones have direct effects on feelings can lift the
postpartum depression or eliminate the need to mourn after wean-
ing has taken place.

To some extent, the emotional consequences of hormonal
changes cannot be separated from situational changes, since all
hormonal changes bring about modifications in the woman's body
and, therefore, often in her life situation. There is always a previous self whose passing one can mourn: for a postpartum woman,
the disappearance of the pregnant self or the loss of that physical
closeness; for some menstruating women, the period as a signal
that she has failed to conceive; for other menstruating women,
simply an inconvenience or a reminder that she regularly must deal
with the hormonal changes in her body and the increase she may
experience in irritability, depression or physical discomfort.

For the adolescent girl, the hormonal changes and their consequences (both the easily observable effects and the changes in
aggressive drive) signal the end of her childhood, the passing of
what she has always been and the coming of an uncertain future.
Except for cases of illness, her body has just undergone the greatest series of changes in her life that she could not attribute either to
someone else (e.g., her parents putting her on a diet) or, more
disturbingly, to her own initiative. This may further increase her
need to take command of herself by trying to identify causes for
her feelings other than the incomprehensible, uncontrollable
changes dictated by her body. Believing her mother is infuriating
her, rather than that her increased aggressive drive makes her respond more explosively than she used to, is somehow reassuring.
In addition, it absolves her of some blame. For girls in particular,
who have learned to suppress anger and aggression, the realization
that they now feel angrier than they used to is tantamount to acknowledging that deep down inside they are "bad."

The third obstacle to acknowledging the effect of hormonally
based changes in feelings is related to the normal, healthy adolescent task of separating from one's parents. A good and a close
relationship with the parents is painful to give up. Even if the
relationship has not been fulfilling for the adolescent, it is painful
and frightening to separate; the adolescent must give up the wish

that someday those needs will be met, and must confront the fact of becoming an adult and taking control of one's own life while feeling unprepared, insecure and cheated. The number of adolescents for whom (and for whose parents) the process of separation is smooth and graceful is very small. Indeed, some clinicians believe that an apparently painless separation indicates a denial of some underlying problems in the family or that the separation never really took place psychologically.

In attempting to understand this third obstacle, let us consider the possible relationship between the task of adolescent separation from the parents and the pubertal increase in sexual and aggressive feelings.

Adolescents often use changes in drive strength for purposes of separation. The need to find outlets for sexual feeling forces the adolescent out of the nuclear family, and, conversely, the need to feel separate often takes the route of sexual activity as a means of achieving or "proving" this separation. But in order to achieve a separation, adolescents must feel they are in control of their bodies and emotions. If they feel too far out of control, they hesitate to form social relationships for fear they will have no control over what will happen. This is one cause of the common adolescent shyness. Most adolescents find it disturbing to have to attribute changes in their feelings to bodies with which they are uncomfortable or dissatisfied. After all, the body is mostly beyond control. "It" makes their voices crack at the worst time, causes erections in embarrassing situations, gives them large or small breasts against their wishes, gives them acute uterine cramps that make them wince visibly in geometry class.

They are then faced with a dilemma. Whom, or what, to trust? Certainly not their own bodies. In some cases, they choose their parents: parental rules might be ridiculous or oppressive, but at least they are usually predictable. Frequently, however, adolescents express their frustration and confusion in the form of anger at their parents. In the following section, we shall examine specific issues that spark the daughter's conflicts with her mother.

Mother as Intruder and Mirror

In the midst of this process, the adolescent girl often finds that she is most often, when home, in the company of her mother. At this time, her belief that her mother can read her thoughts becomes more frightening than ever before. Many people have pointed out how difficult it can be for a daughter living in the house with her father when she reaches adolescence, since his presence arouses her Oedipal-sexual feelings. This is true, but what is often even harder for the daughter to deal with is her feeling that her mother *knows*.

The daughter may believe that a man can be fooled, that she can play games with him that veil her true feelings, but her mother is a different story: she is another female, one who has herself been through a Western female adolescence and typically is the very person who has overtly or implicitly taught the daughter the methods of handling men and hiding feelings. Therefore, in some sense, when the daughter has sexual feelings or expresses her sexuality, her mother is there. She is an automatic intruder into the girl's mental life.

Friday, who has written extensively about women's sexual fantasies, notes (1977) that a common fantasy among females is of their mother walking in while they are masturbating. But calling this a fantasy does not describe the nature of the daughter's feelings, which may be any or all of the following. There is the fear that her mother knows too much: here, it may not be that the daughter is afraid of her mother's actual entry into the room; rather, the imagined scene represents her belief that her mother somehow already "knows" she is masturbating. The fantasy might also be a consequence of the daughter's primary love object having been her mother; hence her mother would be associated with physically pleasant experiences. In this case, the specter of homosexuality, with the likelihood of intense ambivalence, will probably be present at some conscious or unconscious level. Another feeling involved in the fantasy concerns loneliness. People often masturbate when they are lonely. Since thinking of mother—a real or imagined loving mother—is another way to combat loneliness, feel more secure, return to the very earliest ideal or idealized stage of the mother-daughter relationship, masturbation and thoughts of mother may come to be associated.

A girl in adolescence may reject her father because he *arouses* sexual feelings in her, but it is even worse that her mother *understands*. Accordingly, the daughter must reject her mother, pull away from her in the hope that distance will make it harder for her mother to know her feelings.

This sense of her mother's understanding is all the more disturbing for the daughter in adolescence, because adolescence is the stage at which children are supposed to become independent of their parents.

The adolescent girl, then, finds herself in the following situation. There are social pressures, emanating from a biological basis, toward her becoming independent. There are also biologically based pressures toward her expressing and fulfilling her sexuality. At the same time, among the cognitive-emotional baggage that she brings with her from childhood is the belief that her mother can more or less read her mind. What she expects her mother to read there includes sexual feelings that society (and often her mother as well) has told her she must suppress. Social pressures work against biological impulses, and the mother is the awful agent on both sides of the conflict: she knows that the biological impulses exist, and she is likely to have been the most ardent suppressor of them in her daughter.

De Beauvoir (1969) wrote of the relationship between her mother and herself when she was a child growing into adolescence: "I wanted my ramparts to be impregnable. I was particularly diligent in giving away nothing to Maman, out of fear of the distress and horror of having her peer into me." (p. 60) Rich (1976) wrote: "But at the edge of adolescence, we find ourselves drawing back from our natural mother. . . ." (p. 255) She attributes this in part to adolescent girls' incorporation of society's deprecation of women, but the fear of the mother's understanding/intrusiveness is often a contributing factor.

Rich also quotes the words of Aurelia Plath, mother of the poet Sylvia Plath: "Between Sylvia and me existed—as between my own mother and me—a sort of psychic osmosis which, at times, was very wonderful and comforting: at other times an unwelcome invasion of privacy." (p. 230)

The poet Phyllis McGinley wrote a poem called "Girl's-Eye View of Relatives," in her book, *Times Three* (1960) which included the following lines:

A mother's hardest to forgive.

Life is the fruit she longs to hand you,
Ripe on a plate. And while you live,
Relentlessly she understands you. (p. 44)

The daughter feels she lives with a human mirror that will not retreat respectfully into shadow. Her mother is her mirror. Anne Sexton wrote: "A woman *is* her mother. That's the main thing" (1961, p. 48). Perhaps this is one of Sexton's meanings.

Vanity is often attributed to women: *Vanity, thy name is woman!* Women are said to be always glancing at themselves in mirrors. In Michel Tremblay's play *Hosanna*, one of the ways the audience comes to forget that the main character is male is that he is frequently checking his appearance in a mirror. None of this need surprise us when we put together the daughter's experience of living with a mirror/mother, as well as the female role of sex object in which appearance is crucially important. The mother/mirror aspect of the daughter-mother relationship presents the daughter with a mirror whether or not she wishes to look in it, whether or not she would choose to have her mother as a standard of judgment, a reflection of her behavior. The sex-object role makes it necessary for the daughter to initiate the gazing, to check up on her appearance.

Although the adolescent daughter is cognitively able to realize that her mother probably cannot read her mind, she takes a greater risk than ever before if she ignores this possibility. Why? Because the thoughts now in her mind are more and more the kind that her mother, as society's representative and as her earliest, closest companion, has forbidden. They involve sex, anger, rage, activity, aggression, independence. The strict limitations on free exchange of information and feelings about such topics between young girls become destructive. Many adolescent girls cannot check out whether their feelings and experiences are normal or common because they fear that their potential confidante, also being female, would be as shocked and disgusted as their mothers would be.

A mother's knowledge of what her daughter feels is a potential source of comfort to the daughter. But if the daughter's fear of her mother's disapproval is too great, it can be a source of fear and shame.

Mother as Role Model

What is the effect on the adolescent girl of her mother's presence when she looks for a role model in learning to deal with sexual and aggressive feelings? Both these categories of feeling have been considered unacceptable, inappropriate, shocking, even psycho-pathological when straightforwardly acknowledged and expressed by females. But women are supposed to retain and cultivate enough of their sexuality so that men find them appealing and so that they can enjoy sex enough to please their men. Thus a delicate balance must be maintained. A similar pattern holds for aggressive feelings. Women are supposed to channel their aggression care-fully into such routes as manipulation, pretense and scheming in order to "get" and "keep" their men. But they must do all these things without *apparent* effort.

Among the negative consequences of the mother's position as the model for coping with sexuality and aggression is, first of all, the resentment that one typically feels toward such a standard. Any frustration the daughter experiences in her efforts to become like her mother may cause her to associate her mother with that frustration. The child senses that if her mother did not do things quite so well, it would be easier to imitate her. This association tends to be more upsetting for a girl than for a boy (in his relation-ship with his father) because the girl is learning that females are not supposed to feel angry, aggressive, resentful or competitive; hence the girl must suppress or repress her irritation with her mother. Little girls often do this so successfully that their anger does not appear until adolescence, in the form of "unexplainable" or "unjustified" irritability, or deprecation of or rebelliousness against the mother. In some cases, this anger never appears in an overt form but is covered by the daughter's chummy, even con-spiratorial alliance with the mother in which topics of conversation are confined to superficialities or to the safe expression of anger against the daughter's or mother's husband or against men in gen-eral. This latter allows an outlet for anger but ensures that the object of the anger is never the mother.

It is difficult for the mother not to represent some standard of achievement. Even a mother who is not herself traditionally feminine may represent certain standards. Although she may try to teach her daughter to feel free to express feelings and to seek fulfillment of sexual desires, society still discourages such behavior for the daughter. The mother may appear to her daughter to occupy a less vulnerable position. After all, by being a mother she has in some measure propitiated society, and if she is also a wife she has achieved still more propitiation: society is, in some sense, off her back, and she has acceptable routes for channeling at least her sexual expression. But the daughter has not yet filled society's feminine ideal slot of motherhood, and she still struggles between society's insistence on suppression of her feelings and the insistence of her body and mind on their expression.

Both father and mother sometimes hold up the mother as the ideal example of how the daughter should behave, even while mother and daughter compete for the approval of the father. The father's approval and attention often become the signal that the females of the house are "feminine enough." If only by virtue of being younger, smaller and in many ways less skilled and experienced, the daughter suffers by this comparison. Even if she does not suffer in fact, she believes, or sometimes needs to believe, that she does. Smith (1978) describes her relationship with her parents and her parents' relationship with each other as follows:

> . . . the one thing on which my father and mother *did* agree was that I should grow up to be a *lady*. In fact, the path to adulthood in my house was marked by admonitions of behavior. A lady didn't smoke in the street. A lady didn't allow herself to get sunburned. A lady didn't sit with her legs apart, nor notice the vulgarity when her brothers snickered and called it "taking your picture." A lady didn't swear, of course, nor did she drink anything stronger than an occasional glass of wine. A lady didn't interrupt. It drove me berserk. (p. 100)

Later, Smith describes some changes that occurred after her father died: "I had definitely been Daddy's girl. In the time I spent at home after my father's death I received a kind of great awakening and a gift—the full realization of my mother's worth, her wonder, her splendor. . . . I have had the most incredibly fulfilling relationship with my mother since then." (p. 101) Even though she had thought of herself as accepted and specially treated by her father, some competition or tension between herself and her mother disappeared when he was no longer present.

To a teenaged girl who feels frightened, gawky, confused and inept, the belief that her mother is perfect may leave her feeling hopeless about tackling the tasks at hand. She may feel jealous or furious with her mother for setting such a high standard and performing nonchalantly the tasks that she herself finds overwhelming. Such a mother often conveys societal prohibitions against sexual and aggressive activity to her daughter while appearing to have accepted those rules for herself gracefully, painlessly, even willingly. Such a daughter wonders hopelessly how she can ever manage to bring under control the feelings that seem to push relentlessly for expression. She may feel a growing certainty around this time that her own intense needs are abnormal: surely no women— not even her mother—could have managed to control them so well if they, too, had experienced them.

What happens if the mother is an inadequate model? In such a case, imitating her mother's behavior does not bring the daughter the approval of others and may even elicit the disapproval of the inadequate mother herself, who is angry that her little girl brings her shame in the eyes of society. A daughter who cannot learn from her mother how to earn the approval and warmth of others finds herself feeling ambivalent. In one respect, she is victorious: she is a better woman than her mother and may win her father's preference for her over her mother. But it is a sad victory, because it gives her too much power. Children who feel they have more power than their parents become afraid of their impulses; they have in some sense destroyed (or replaced) their own mother. Thus, in fact or in fantasy, they lose the love of their primary love object, the mother. They incur her wrath or at least the withdrawal of nurturance that characterizes mothers who feel they have failed in their maternal roles. In addition, a mother who has not shown her daughter how to attract males will probably be the object of her adolescent daughter's fury and deprecation.

Sheehy (1976) illustrates how a daughter who skillfully carries out the traditional female tasks because her mother cannot, or does not, comes to feel guilty for surpassing the mother:

    ". . . Mother always going out on some pretense of grocery shopping; Dad literally dragging her out of bars. Whenever I was home I had to work, diapering, vacuuming, cooking, being a second mother to my brothers and sisters. I got into a terrible competition with my mother because I was more patient and clever at managing the little ones. She would yell and scream." Ginny felt smug but always guilty; she had replaced her mother in a role on which the mother had defaulted. (pp. 220–21)

But what about a mother who is still clearly struggling to channel her own sexual and aggressive feelings in socially acceptable ways? She may be an intentional rebel against societal standards, or she may wish to conform but find herself for various reasons unable to do so. The mother who wishes to conform but cannot presents to her daughter a weakness that the daughter may find disconcerting. Crucial to a satisfactory outcome of adolescent struggles is the background of at least one strong parent figure. Just as the jumps on a trampoline go more surely, more gracefully, when the trampoline is taut, so the adolescent needs a strong parent against whom to compare the experiments and fluctuations of adolescence. A mother who cannot do what she is trying to teach her daughter to do provides too weak a background. Her daughter can have little confidence in her advice (If you're so smart, why ain't you rich?) and has little to learn from imitating the mother's unsuccessful attempts to conform.

For a mother who does not accept the norms of society for female's behavior, the story is a little different. In *Of Woman Born* (1976), the poet Adrienne Rich says that she was relieved to have had only sons because she is a feminist and would have wanted to raise her daughters according to the feminist principles. She believed that she would have been apprehensive, realizing that the daughter would have to be strong indeed in order to confront a society that still resists nonconformity in its women. It is one thing to decide to face such issues oneself and to be willing to suffer the consequences. But it is more difficult to give birth to a child knowing one is throwing her into a life for which she must be exceedingly strong and self-confident, and being unsure of one's ability to help her develop such strength. If this concern is not explained compassionately to the daughter, it may produce in her an apprehensiveness the origins of which she does not understand and cannot, therefore, overcome.

Mother as Source of Restrictions

In adolescence, the dormant specter of the mother who imposes society's restrictions on the daughter is often vigorously revived. This is because of the adolescent's increase in feelings of sexuality and aggression. As society's representative and the guardian of her child's well-being and reputation (and thereby of her own), the mother is likely to become anxious to suppress those feelings in her daughter. Not only the daughter's changed feelings but also her new physical vulnerability (soft breasts that may be injured, a womb that may be impregnated) justify increased concern on the mother's part. But this concern may be misused by mothers who become overly protective, overanxious or even aggressive. Some mothers, uneasy about their daughters' increasingly obvious sexuality, as well as their capacity for aggression, make contemptuous or derogatory remarks to them. This is sometimes an attempt to force the daughters to believe that they are not yet sexually attractive, to threaten them so that they will hesitate to express their aggression or sexuality.

The mother's position as the continuing source of societal instructions has the following consequences: if the daughter flaunts social propriety, she goes against her mother's instructions and thus mother-daughter conflict arises; if the daughter wants to do what is socially approved, her mother, as the ideal, is resented by the daughter for her "perfection," compared to which the daughter finds her own efforts pitiful; at the very least, the mother may be regarded as the "knower" of what is approved, what is adequate.

The daughter's dependence on her mother for information therefore puts her at her mother's mercy. This is one reason an adolescent turns energetically to her peers: she brings in their opinions, to shore herself up against her underlying belief (and, often, her fear and resentment) that her parents are correct. The daughter who really believes, deep down, in her mother's correctness may find it especially hard to individuate herself from her mother; every decision she makes in the way that her mother would may seem another instance of obedience rather than being separate and independent.

The socially learned need of both mother and daughter to believe that the mother is good and wise may aggravate the situation. Daughters need to believe their mothers are good mothers in order to protect them from society's disapproval; therefore, they find it hard to behave differently from their mothers. They believe this is the "wrong" thing to do, and they fear bringing disgrace upon their mothers by their "misbehavior."

Daughter-Mother Separations

This type of dilemma often remains unresolved by the time the daughter leaves home. Whether she is getting married, going off to college, or simply moving out, insofar as she has come to feel responsible for her mother's happiness she feels guilty about her departure. Having protected her mother's feelings for so long, she worries about how her mother will get along without her. It is here that the mother-daughter role reversal often becomes most clearly apparent. Particularly if the mother has no other work or interests, or has an unsatisfactory relationship with her husband, the daughter may worry more than the mother about how the other will get on. Daughters often describe having felt with certainty that they were the people on whom their mothers could lean, that they gave meaning and hope to their mothers' lives. They tell stories that bring tears to their eyes twenty and thirty years later, of how sad and adrift their mothers looked as they left home. Others tell how their mothers telephoned them three times a week their first year at college; often, the daughters were pleased at first, but once they got over their homesickness they found it irritating and felt guilty for having a good time when their mothers were saying things like "Every time I walk by your old room, I start to cry."

The conflict is particularly severe when the daughter believes that her mother has given up a potential career for the sake of her children; it is aggravated further when there has been hostility between mother and daughter that both parties have denied. The guilt about their unspoken hostility often begins to feed on the daughter, in much the same way that relatives of the deceased feel guilty: "I wasn't as nice as I should have been when I still lived at home, and now it's too late."

Friday (1977) describes the guilt she felt on the occasions when she left her mother: "Suddenly, at the last minute, her [Friday's mother's] face collapsed into that sad wistful look she always had when we parted. 'Oh, Nance,' she began, and reached for me tentatively. I returned her embrace with less warmth than I would have liked, hating myself for not being able to give my mother what she wanted." (p. 258) This example illustrates again the role reversal in which the daughter feels guilty for failing to meet the mother's needs, rather than recognizing that separation is often difficult for both parties. She might have focused on her own sadness about separating, but she found it difficult to shift her focus away from the look on her mother's face.

Friday (1977) asks:

> Can you stand your mother's sadness? We believe that if we had been better children, or even right now could do or say the right thing, we could make it go away. I cannot bear to be in the same room when my mother's face changes from that look I love to that maddening unhappiness. My intellect tells me the guilt I feel whenever I say good-bye to her has nothing to do with what I did or didn't do. My mother is a reasonably happy woman, other people would say. I've been a reasonably good daughter, my mother would say. But until I understand my guilt, I will not be free of her. (p. 28)

Many daughters have mothers who are unhappily married or who have no life except for their families. In such cases, the daughter believes she is the measure of her mother's life because her mother cannot complain about her unhappiness to outsiders; no one else will really understand. If the mother is unhappy with her husband, she is still likely to want to protect him from the disapproval of others. If she is unhappy because her children have grown and left home, and she wishes to work, she may fear that this is inappropriate for a woman and be reluctant to mention it to outsiders. So the daughter senses that her mother can talk to her more easily than to anyone else, and she feels that she should be available to listen to her mother's troubles. If she is not available, there are two worrying possibilities. One is that her mother will remain isolated and miserable, in which case the daughter continues to feel guilty. Another is that the mother will find a new confidante. Particularly for a daughter who has had an unsatisfactory relationship with her mother, this is a frightening thought; she fears that the one sure-fire route to closeness with her mother—that of listening to her problems and supporting her—will be usurped by someone else.

Traditional social norms often aggravate the conflict between the daughter's wish to emancipate herself from her mother and her sense of responsibility for her mother's unhappiness. In some circles, it is considered normal, "cute," certainly acceptable for a mother and daughter to talk on the telephone every day, reporting each small detail of their lives to each other. Thus a daughter who wishes to try to remain in a sympathetic role with respect to her mother often finds that without this daily contact both she and her mother suspect that she really doesn't care enough.

Friday (1977) quotes Sonya Friedman's description of many married women:

> The more I talk to women, the more anger I uncover. All the depression, the going to sleep early, not having energy, the fact that it's three in the afternoon and she's still sitting around in her housecoat —all these are various forms of anger. "I'm bored," she says, "I went through all this schooling, I used to have dreams but now I know they aren't going to be met. I'm even afraid to go back to school, to get out there and compete." Most of the anger has to do with the way she was raised. Marriage, she was told, would be the answer to all problems. (p. 360)

Who, in most cases, tells the daughter that marriage will be such an answer? Usually it is the mother, and so the daughter comes to feel angry toward her. But the daughter understands, whether consciously or not, that her mother did this in part to justify her own life and in part on the instructions of society. In addition, because women are not supposed to show anger, the anger that a daughter feels toward her mother is suppressed or repressed.

When anger is dealt with in this way, the daughter comes to sense that she is not wholehearted in her pleasure at seeing her mother. This makes the times of separation particularly difficult, because even though to an onlooker she might appear to treat her mother lovingly during a visit, the anger has been a barrier between them and the daughter has not felt relaxed. She has had to be vigilant, lest her anger slip out against her will, and this has caused restraint in her interactions with her mother. Therefore, when the time comes for mother and daughter to part, some of the daughter's guilt is due to her sense that she has not given as much as she might have, even if her mother seemed not to notice.

The Daughter's Search for Identity

A crucial task of the adolescent is to develop an identity separate from those of the parents. This is particularly difficult for the daughter searching for an identity that will be different from her mother's. In a major respect, it is more difficult than for a son who is trying to establish an identity different from that of his father. The reason is that females' role options are traditionally much more restricted than those of males. Erikson, whose theory of the "identity crisis" in adolescence has been important in understanding this stage of development, has asserted that the identity of a female is mostly defined by "whom she decides to admit to her inner space," that is, whom she will marry, who will make her pregnant, fill her womb (Erikson, 1968). Ayim (1977) has suggested that the three primary roles allowed to women have been those of "wife, mother and bait," the last of these indicating her role as an ornamental object designed to attract and "hook" a man.

What this means for the growing girl, compared to the growing boy, is illustrated by the following examples. The son of a lawyer father can decide to become a physician, a college professor, a professional baseball player, a businessman—any of hundreds of occupations that meet the criteria of being consistent with the traditional male image as active, assertive, influential in various ways. The son can choose an occupation different from his father's but still fit many of the same descriptive terms. He can identify with his father but choose a work identity that indicates both his continuing "maleness" and also his separateness. If he chooses to work at the same type of job in the same place as his father, he will not be making that choice simply because any other would be "unmasculine."

It is more difficult for a daughter and her mother. The daughter of a housewife has traditionally been able to choose to be a housewife. Sometimes she has chosen teaching or nursing, which are forms of child-related and caretaking work that society considers

close enough to housekeeping to fit the definition of "feminine," or
sometimes secretarial or other office work, which has usually re-
quired that she in various ways "take care" of her male boss and
which was defined more by the name and identity of her boss or the
organization than by its nature. But even for women who have
worked outside their homes, the connotations that "spinster" has
had as contrasted to "bachelor" reflect the fact that, even if a
woman had a vocation, the crucial aspect of her "feminine" identity has been her role as wife and mother. Few ways have thus
been left for her to come to feel different from her mother while
still remaining traditionally "feminine." This has seriously complicated the process for the adolescent daughter of developing a
strong sense of her own identity.

Raphael (1978) has noted this disturbingly close association of
the mother's accomplishments (or lack thereof) with the daughter's, though she does not attempt to explain its basis: ". . . our
mothers' failings are implicitly our own. We're scared, we're
threatened, we're angry and we're disappointed because if they're
not perfect, we're not perfect." (p. 179)

Rich (1976) discusses women's attitudes about being like their
mothers. She says of Virginia Woolf's young woman character
Lily Briscoe's feelings about her idol Mrs. Ramsay: "She does not
want to *be* Mrs. Ramsay, and her discovery of this is crucial for
her." (p. 237) This illustrates the claustrophobic quality that many
girls and women discover when trying to find identities with which
they feel comfortable and of which they can also feel proud. The
limitations on acceptable roles available for women have left them
so few choices that it sometimes seems hard not to swallow whole
the role of another. One hears many women and girls today saying,
"X is a wonderful woman, and I want to be exactly like her." Boys
and men also have idols and people they regard as ideal, but the
finding of an idol or a role model for a woman is more difficult.
Interpreted at one very simple level, the paucity of interesting role
models for women has meant that developing females have had
less practice at separating and recombining desirable aspects of
various women with each other.

Daughter-Mother Anger

Given the dilemmas and conflicts of adolescence discussed so far, it is clear that it would be helpful if the daughter could express some of her anger and frustration. Her male peers can do this in sports activities, half-joking wrestling and punching matches, use of obscene language, throwing spitballs in class, staying out past curfew, acting out sexually, not informing parents of their where-abouts or plans. But all of these outlets traditionally have been either barred to females officially (as in the case of school sports) or defined as unfeminine. In fact, such types of behavior as sexual acting out, breaking curfew and running away, which have tended to bring females into juvenile courts, constitute behavior that has been tolerated far more in boys. Recent books that counsel women to serve their husbands and be infinitely pliable, attractive sex objects for them, give women the following advice about how to use "anger" for seduction: "Beat your little hands in impotent rage against his chest."

Not only expression of anger but also competition is forbidden to women, at least in straightforward forms. Competition between two women for the same man is acceptable in certain forms but is not considered attractive or appropriate between mother and daughter; hence any indications of mother-daughter jealousy or competitiveness are usually frightening and upsetting to both parties, and attempts are made to suppress or deny them: "Me jealous of my mother? Hah! Are you kidding?" Or: "I only borrow my daughter's miniskirts when nothing of my own is handy." Thus, even if a daughter could freely choose to be a housewife like her mother, she would still have trouble establishing her own separate identity. Perhaps this explains the intense pride women may take in waxing their floors until they outshine their mothers' or their neigh-bors' floors. It is certainly a part of the destructive mothering that is reflected in mothers' fierce pushing of their children into compe-tition for cutest baby pictures, best Girl Scout, prettiest cheer-leader or most sought-after member of a high school sorority.

The Daughter's Ambivalence About Her Mother

The adolescent upsurge in sexual feelings revives a conflict about parents that the daughter probably experienced in childhood. This conflict sometimes includes a confusion or juxtaposition of her sexual feelings and her wishes for warmth and security. She still feels (whether unconsciously or consciously) drawn toward her mother, who was her primary love object and who often remains emotionally closer to her than does her father. Psychoanalytic theory suggests that the girl's sexual feelings for her father, which were active in early childhood, are reawakened in her adolescence and that she finds this both attractive and frightening. In part because of this and in part because of her increasingly adult sexual feelings and physical appearance, her father may in one respect seem more threatening to her than her mother, since her mother cannot physically invade her as her father potentially can. The daughter seesaws between feeling that her mother is a greater threat to her own identity and, on the other hand, feeling that her father is actually or potentially more intrusive (emotionally and, not as rarely as was formerly believed, even physically) because his maleness arouses sexual feelings that she is struggling to control. Despite the incest taboo, the father's maleness renders him more similar to the male peers she can now at least flirt with, if not acceptably become more sexually involved with. With her mother, the experiencing of sexual feelings is more likely to be at a deeper level, much farther from the girl's awareness, because of the threat of homosexuality.

The seesaw continues with the daughter's feelings toward her mother. The daughter seeks the warmth her mother represents and then is repelled by it, because it can seduce her back to the role of child or infant, inhibiting her emotional growth, and because it ultimately may arouse homosexual feelings. All of this is aggravated still further by the traditional father's less expressive style than his wife's, which, combined with his greater absence from home, leaves his relationship with his daughter more distant than the mother-daughter relationship. Mother and daughter, more than father and daughter, encounter each other at every turn, and every turn is a potential source of conflict.

The intensity with which the daughter may be attracted by her mother as an image of warmth and security depends to some extent on whether the mother was able to offer adequate nurturance during the daughter's infancy and early childhood. If she was, then the attractiveness of such security is not intensified by the fantasies the inadequately nurtured daughter feels—that perhaps someday her mother will be loving enough to make her feel finally secure and strong. An adequately nurtured daughter will have developed enough strength based on that early experience that she can look forward to further growth and development.

Although it virtually never comes into consciousness at this stage, the increase in sexual feelings that comes with puberty makes the homosexual pull toward the mother stronger and harder for the girl to resist. Her mother was most likely her original love object, the source of most of the pleasure she experienced during her very early life, no matter how much or little pleasure that was. Now, with an increased drive toward sexual pleasure, it would be surprising if the girl did not find her mother an attractive object for the drive, even though the attraction is probably unconscious. When it is consciously acknowledged, the attraction usually takes the form of a wish to be a little girl and have mother take care of her, so that she would not have to cope with the adolescent tasks of learning to deal with sexuality and aggression.

Freud considered infants capable of experiencing a wide variety of pleasure, which he often called sexual or libidinous pleasure. For our purposes, it is more helpful to follow Klein's suggestion (1969), and think in terms of the mother being considered a source of sensuous pleasure—pleasure that one feels through one's senses, including touch, smell and sight. Even if we wish to disregard the view that the mother arouses unconscious homosexual feelings in her adolescent daughter, it is clear that the mother often represents sensuous pleasure to her daughter. The daughter's experiences in infancy of her mother as a giver of pleasure receive added force from the social stereotype of women as loving to wear soft clothes, smell nice, be treated gently so that they feel good, and be protected from the unpleasantnesses of the world outside the cozy home. It is an image that conflicts with the woman-as-all-enduring and nurturing image, with which it coexists. But an adolescent daughter seeking to fulfill her increased needs for sexual pleasure often finds that the former social stereotype helps her to regard her mother as a member of the elite group of adults who understand and experience sensual and sexual pleasure. She is likely to feel a mixture of resentment and jealousy of her mother for having such lovely secrets and experiences, and also admiration and a wish to be like her. At the same time, her attraction to her mother may be increased by her admiration for the things for which her mother stands. Society has come to expect and accept what it calls "adolescent crushes," but the fear of homosexuality usually makes admiration and attraction for one's mother seem unacceptable. Thus this crush is typically displaced onto another adult female who can be regarded as an idol rather than an object of attraction; someone else's mother, or a teacher, or a movie star has not shared with the adolescent a history of the giving and receiving of closeness and physical pleasure.

Menstruation

The beginning of menstruation can create difficulties between mother and daughter by calling forth the feelings that either or both of them have about two issues: that of toilet training or general control and that of sexuality. Today, the situation is better than it used to be, when even in the previous one or two generations menstruation often took girls by surprise and terror because their mothers could not bring themselves to discuss it. But even mothers who have truthfully informed their daughters about the facts of menstruation may find it hard to conceal the intensity of their anxieties about it. Western societies have begun to dictate that we must give our daughters information so they will not feel frightened or sinful when the menstrual blood appears. Still, it takes more than factual education to rid mothers and daughters of the various anxieties this event can provoke.

Writing about menstruation, de Beauvoir (1974) observes:

> All the evidence agrees in showing that whether the child has been forewarned or not, the event always seems to her repugnant and humiliating. Frequently her mother has neglected to inform her; it has been noted that mothers more readily explain to their daughters the mysteries of pregnancy, childbirth, and even sexual relations than the facts of menstruation. They themselves seem to abhor this feminine burden. . . . Even if wise instruction spares her too vivid anxiety, the girl feels ashamed, soiled. . . . (pp. 348–49)

The menstrual flow comes without being willed to come. It is a part of a woman's physiology but is beyond her conscious control. Although advertisements for tampons are increasingly public and forthright, they usually reflect the panic most women feel that a spot of blood might seep through their skirt and be seen by others. Many women and girls feel about this possibility nearly the same as they would about public notice if they wet or soiled themselves. After early childhood, one learns, the inability to control the products of one's body means that one is inadequate, weak, stupid, filthy or even evil. When we consider the intense reluctance American teenagers feel about raising their hands in class in case drops of sweat should show on their shirts' underarms, we begin to appreciate how much adolescents and adults fear to reveal bodily products more nearly associated with sexuality or, in the minds of some, excretion. Sweat at least may come from healthy exercise, despite its possible sexual associations, but menstruation is clearly sexual and comes from the general area of the female body that even most females associate with the excretion for which they learn to feel disgust. Girls and women sense that during menstrual periods they must use tampons, pads and deodorant sprays with exquisite care so that others will not be exposed to their "unpleasantness."

Thus we see yet another manifestation of the traditional female concern to protect the sensibilities of others.

The intensity of some young women's fear of a slip-up in this vigilance may lead to interesting but disturbing behavior. One very pretty, popular sixteen-year-old girl who was known for her "femininity" and friendliness described her behavior and reasoning when her menstrual blood stained the back of her skirt: "I discovered the spot at noon and was horrified. I considered going home to change, but then people would know that I knew the spot was there, and they might think I had known it was there for awhile before I changed my skirt. So I went through the rest of the day in the spotted skirt. I figured that people would think I had not realized the spot was there." This girl felt that, though it might be embarrassing for others to see the blood, it would have been much worse for them to assume she knew but did not immediately remove it—better to be thought fastidious though unaware than aware and not instantly fastidious. The nearness to panic that so many females feel in this respect suggests that their concern is connected to the early life event of toilet training, since it suggests shame about loss of control and "dirt."

The anxieties of both daughters and mothers converge when their eyes meet as mother hands daughter her first sanitary pad. They are both aware that their reputations for cleanliness and femininity depend on the daughter learning to protect others from the sight and smell of her new blood.

When menstruation begins, the girl's sexuality has undeniably arrived. In fact, menstruation is often the first sudden, dramatic proof of her sexuality. It means a new vulnerability for the girl, because she may now become pregnant, and therefore signifies her unavoidable arrival at several choice points—including whether to be a mother, like her own mother, and whether to consider her ability to become pregnant a summation of what her life will be. This is also frequently a time of conflict between daughter and mother: the daughter's need for information from her mother can clash with her need for self-confidence and a sense of pride, ownership and control over her sexuality. Depending on how the mother dealt with these same issues during and after her own adolescence, the mother may feel inadequate to the task of giving her daughter information and may feel angry about this and jealous of her daughter's youth.

Competition Between Daughter and Mother

As the daughter becomes clearly a sexual being, the potential for competition between mother and daughter is intensified. Whether or not one accepts psychoanalytic theories about the revival of the Oedipal conflict in adolescence, there is no doubt that the father is usually the man for whose attention and approval mother and daughter begin to compete. He is there, he often wields a great deal of power in the family, and, being male, his opinions are probably highly valued. The daughter often feels that she cannot compete with her mother's womanliness, and the mother often wonders whether her daughter's youthful attractiveness makes her husband realize how much she has aged. These conflicts are extremely painful for mothers and daughters to admit because they involve what has been one of the two cardinal aspects of traditional femininity, i.e., sexual attractiveness (the other being nurturance).

De Beauvoir (1974) describes what happens when the daughter appears to become a sexual being:

> Many a mother hardens into hostility; she does not accept being supplanted by the ingrate who owes her her life. The jealousy felt by the coquette toward the fresh adolescent girl who shows up her artifice has often been noted: she who has seen a hated rival in every woman will see the same even in her own child: she sends her away or keeps her out of sight, or she contrives to deprive her of social opportunities. She who took pride in being the Wife, the Mother, in exemplary and unique fashion, none the less fights dethronement fiercely. She goes on saying her daughter is only a child, she regards her undertakings as juvenile games; she is too young to marry, too delicate to procreate. If she persists in wanting a husband, a home, children, all this will never be more than make-believe. The mother never wearies of criticizing, deriding, or predicting trouble. If allowed to do so, she condemns her daughter to eternal childhood; if not, she tries to ruin the adult life the other is bold enough to claim. (p. 654)

Interestingly, some research (Caplan et al., 1979) has shown that of delinquent girls and boys referred to a clinic for psychological assessment, the girls were far more likely than the boys to have older mothers. One possible explanation for this finding is that the age of the girls' mothers caused them to be more threatened by their daughters' entering adolescence and becoming attractive young women. The competition between mother and daughter may have been one cause of the daughter's illegal behavior. Also consistent with this explanation is the finding that the girls' "crimes" were more likely to involve self-destructive or escapist behavior. This would not be surprising if the girls felt guilty (probably unconsciously) for being young and attractive and thereby outdoing their mothers; their delinquent behavior could then be interpreted as an attempt to punish themselves for making their mothers unhappy. Their escapist behavior might have been an adaptive reaction in some cases to a real situation: their fathers in fact found them more attractive than their mothers, and this frightened them.

The question of competition between mother and daughter for the father's attention and approval is an extremely delicate one.

There are so many ways in which things can go wrong. A mother who has apparently been successful in becoming an attractive, self-confident woman can unintentionally make her daughter feel inadequate: I could never be like my mother, so why should I even try? This is an especially upsetting feeling for an adolescent girl since women's role limitations have allowed fewer arenas in which a daughter can succeed while still being "acceptably feminine." If the mother is clearly unsuccessful at being attractive and self-confident, or if the family psychodynamics are such that the daughter feels she has won her father's attention away from her mother, she is likely to feel guilty and frightened. Along with these feelings often goes a sense of omnipotence, of being able to make something happen by wishing for it, or the belief that she deserves to have anything she wants and can do as she pleases. And if the world doesn't like it, something is wrong with the world.

A mother who is self-confident and who has encouraged her daughter to develop aspects of herself aside from her physical attractiveness and seductiveness will avoid some of the unnecessarily intense effects described above. A society that promoted such breadth of development in females would also help a great deal. But some of the phenomena noted in the previous paragraphs are likely to appear in the normal adolescence of most young girls. As with most of the subject matter in this book, the concern is with exaggerations of normal processes and with creation or perpetuation of these extremes by the traditions that have restricted women's roles.

The Issue of Death

There are several aspects of the effect of the issue of death on the relationship between the mother and the adolescent daughter. One is related to the role of the mother in restricting her daughter's behavior. As noted, the adolescent girl experiences an upsurge in sexual and aggressive drives, which brings her into conflict with the established rules for adolescent girls' behavior. Thus adolescence is a time when the girl confronts many limitations: those imposed by her own body, those imposed by society (often through her mother) and, by extension, those of her own mortality.

Though younger children understand the concept of death in certain ways, the adolescent's dramatically increased capacity for abstract and symbolic thinking and planning gives her a new sense of her vulnerability and finiteness, whether conscious or not. This appears to be one reason for adolescents investing much energy in daydreams that do away with limitations and impossibilities: they dream of great accomplishments that the world will never forget, of making an immortal mark, of teaching eternal values. These are means of coping with, denying or trying to work around the meaning of their death. As already discussed, the mother is an easy target for the projection of many forms of anger and anxiety about death, and her role as imposer of restrictions on the daughter's potential in some ways parallels the fact of the death that awaits the daughter. This broadens the mother's position as a target, drawing the fire of all her daughter's fear and anger about the limitations in and on her life, including her death.

Awareness of death can affect the adolescent daughter's relationship with her mother in another way as well. Because of the countless areas in which daughters are expected or assumed to be similar to their mothers ("If you want to know what kind of woman you're marrying, just look at her mother"), the daughter sees her own eventual aging and mortality in her mother's wrinkles and age spots. Any fear, disgust or anger she feels at the thought of her own aging and death is reflected in the signs of age in her mother's face and body. The daughter may learn to fear her mother's aging because she believes it predicts the nature of her own. The image of the mirror again appears: looking at her mother, the daughter may come to believe that she sees there what the future holds in store—the presumed loss of her own value as a woman and her own death.

Adult Daughter and Mother

In discussing the adult stage, I shall consider first the daughter who chooses a conventional "feminine" life of wifehood, pregnancy, childbearing and child-rearing, and then the daughter who chooses less conventional types of activities.

It is commonly believed that mother and daughter become closer when the daughter marries and/or has children of her own. These events sometimes have that effect, of course, and one might even speculate that in most cases an increase in closeness occurs; this would be understandable since the two women would then share some experience in the roles of wife and mother. Before accepting this myth as reality, however, one must recognize that there are at least two potential sources of difficulty when the daughter enters the roles of wife and mother. One involves the issue of competitiveness. No matter how well she believes she has fulfilled her roles, a mother may resent the picture her daughter presents of being an even better wife and mother than she herself has ever been. On the other side of the coin is the daughter who believes erroneously that her mother has happily and effortlessly carried off the roles of wife and mother, and who resents her for it.

The other potential source of difficulty between mother and daughter concerns the arousal, or rearousal, of whatever dissatisfactions the mother has experienced in these roles. If she sees her daughter as happy in the roles of wife and mother, she may resent her for it and believe herself to be inadequately feminine. If the daughter experiences the same kinds of frustrations in these roles that the mother experienced, then knowledge of her daughter's unhappiness can elicit several feelings in the mother. One is guilt, for not having helped her daughter to avoid the traps and limitations that she herself intimately knows. Another is anxiety: if the mother is still trying to suppress and "learn to live with" her own dissatisfactions, then she may regard her daughter uneasily as a reminder of them. Whatever sympathy and concern she has for her daughter will make it difficult to ignore her daughter's dilemmas, and confronting these makes it harder to believe they are not her own. The mother may also feel shame if she believes that her daughter's unhappiness in her new roles is due to a failure on her part to teach her daughter how to be happy in them.

One must not overlook the extent to which similarity of experience can bring women closer together; the effects are not always as described above. Indeed, even societal stereotypes may bring mother and daughter closer at times when stereotypes drive husband and wife apart. Men who have been trained for years not to show tenderness, and who have not been trained to take over the cooking and housekeeping duties when necessary, may find themselves reluctant to look after a wife who is tired or unwell because of her pregnancy. At such times, the wife's mother often tries to fill such needs, since as a woman she has been trained in these tasks. Both husband and mother may care about the pregnant woman, then, but it is the mother's training that prepares her to respond to needs that are a product of her daughter's relationship with her husband.

Generally by definition, or by convention, a daughter's mother was married, and by definition her mother had at least one child. What kind of wife and mother was she? Or, more important for our purposes, what kind of wife and mother did the daughter think she was? Daughters whose mothers seemed to handle these tasks with difficulty, resentment or ambivalence may regard their mothers angrily as providing poor role models for them, as having set a poor example. The woman who recognizes in her own exasperated yelling at her children the same phrases, the same tone of voice that her mother used with her, may attribute her frustrations to her mother's failure to teach her how to cope. Again we think of Anne Sexton's line "A woman *is* her mother. That's the main thing" (Sexton, 1961, p. 48). What makes it so important for a woman's own mother to be the model of wifely and motherly behavior? Why cannot the daughter learn as well from books or from watching other people's mothers, or by acting as differently as possible from the unsatisfactory ways in which her mother behaved?

The answer to this has two parts. One reason lies in the fact that we do not learn only when we are aware that we are learning. We begin to learn styles of behavior, and to associate certain situations with certain feelings, while very, very young. It is then too early for us to stop and think, to separate what we observe from what we learn by repeated experience to feel. When her children fight, the mother seems afraid they are beyond her control, afraid she is failing as a mother. The children sense this and learn to associate the situation of fighting children with the image of poor mothering and with a general feeling of anxiety. The experience of being a small child in a family is intense, enveloping. It is extremely difficult to rid oneself of those early associations between certain situations and the feelings of one's parents at the time they occurred. This makes it easier to learn from one's mother than to learn through other routes, though the latter is not impossible.

The other obstacle that has made it difficult for women to learn wifely and motherly skills from other sources has been the combination of the myths held by society about the perfect serenity and selflessness of motherhood and the consequent isolation of housewives from each other's lives. In 1949, in *Male and Female,* Margaret Mead observed: "Even in our highly diversified society, each small family is so isolated from others that no one knows how peculiar or how usual are the feelings and behaviors that are shut behind each Yale lock. . . ." (p. 113)

This isolation continues to a great degree. One of the major factors working to maintain the isolation of housewives from each other is each individual housewife's belief that every mother except herself is serene. Each is certain that the rage, the physical exhaustion, the desperate wish for two consecutive hours of guiltless privacy are feelings that only she has—feelings unbecoming in a wife and mother—and that her women friends would believe something was disturbed or bad about her if they knew. Another major factor in maintaining this isolation is each woman's dependence on her husband for economic support and continuation of her "respectable" role as wife, one of the requirements of which has traditionally been that each wife shall protect her husband's reputation. Complaining to another woman that one's husband never helps with the children and that one is exhausted, angry and frightened about shouldering the entire responsibility for the children is inconsistent with this protection.

Recently, while lecturing to a rural, politically conservative group of parents, I alluded to what I called "the myth that motherhood is serene." As soon as I had spoken the phrase, I feared that I had chosen the wrong words for my audience, but then I realized they were laughing and applauding. Women are becoming aware that virtually all mothers feel rage, for example, when their infant's or child's needs interfere with their own needs for rest or for stimulation other than that provided by the child. The regional mothers' groups now being formed to give new mothers the support and sharing of information about the realities of motherhood can help to combat the stereotypes of total unselfishness and freedom from boredom that motherhood is popularly thought to imply. Ideally, these groups will include fathers as well, since they are modern substitutes for the now rare extended family that used to provide new parents such information and support.

The isolation of women from each other's experiences and reactions has made them more dependent than necessary on their own early experiences in the nuclear family, on what they learned at their mother's knee. The daughter trying to raise a family may find herself repeating her mother's failures and thus nourishing a festering resentment of her mother. Part of this process that is often overlooked involves the awareness of the adult daughter that her mother is not as wonderful as she had thought—or, even more commonly, not wonderful in *the same ways* as she had thought. It may come in a flash: Even my mother is not selfless, slim and serene! The fact that the daughter has often presented her mother to society as a mother beyond reproach makes it even more difficult to confront this reality. Who will defend mother if not I? How can I risk bringing down upon my mother the disapproval of society? Talking to others about their mothers' imperfections becomes as difficult as talking about their husbands' failings. When people realize that someone close to them is not what they have always believed, a kind of mourning is appropriate, a grieving for the loss of the "person I thought she was." The daughter's fear of the intensity of her own anger about such a realization combined with the necessity of protecting the mother's reputation further isolates the daughter; and if she allows herself to mourn, she usually mourns alone.

Isolation of women has a similarly destructive effect on adult daughters who become wives and mothers, and whose own mothers seem to have performed easily the wife and mother roles. It is rare that anyone, male or female, finds marriage or child-raising easy. A mother whose child has not been aware of the difficulties, dilemmas or problems that needed solving becomes afraid to admit even to herself that she has problems and unpleasant times. Such a mother teaches her daughter through her own behavior that problems are to be denied or sailed through. This comes partly from her fear that to look as though being a wife and mother is difficult would suggest that she is unfeminine, dissatisfied with her role. The daughter of such a woman tends to regard herself as emotionally disturbed, unusually prone to anger, "unfeminine" or "bitchy" when she finds that she does not smoothly negotiate the real problems. She resents the mother for having "protected" her from reality and thus having left her unprepared to be a wife and mother. This lack of preparation, the lack of exposure to a coping, problem-solving wife and mother who is fallible enough to feel everyday frustrations, can be as destructive to a daughter as the lack of information about sex and sexuality. The daughter may feel even more isolated from her "perfect" mother than from other women, at a time when she most needs to turn to her for advice, information and sharing of feelings.

We now turn to the daughter who, in addition to or instead of becoming a wife and mother, has a career of her own. If her employment is aimed only at bringing in more money for the financially struggling family, then if she has a traditional mother, mother and daughter may not clash over the question of whether the daughter should work. But conflicts often arise between them if the daughter's work has some other aim (such as self-improvement, advancement of her career for its own sake or simply her own enjoyment and independence).

A growing number of mothers warmly support their daughters' efforts to become independent and to advance in their vocations. Toward daughters who work for enjoyment and self-development, however, the mothers' attitudes may be encouraging, disapproving or some combination of the two. Mothers' strongest feelings about their daughters' work or career is often complicated by other feelings as well. One type of mother supports her daughter's achievement from childhood; she tells her daughter that her efforts are good, urges her on to greater accomplishments. If such a mother has made achievements of her own outside her home—in an office or in the community—the following pattern is not uncommon. The mother is proud of her small daughter's accomplishments and boasts about them to others, almost as though they were her own. But as the child enters adolescence or adulthood, the mother comes to regard the daughter's achievements as threatening: she may be (or may believe she will be) overshadowed by them. In such cases, the mother displays an ambivalent attitude toward the adult daughter's work, sometimes continuing to feel as though it were somehow her own and other times feeling threatened by it, fearing her daughter as a competitor. This is a situation fairly commonly encountered by fathers and sons, and it is painful for them as well, but for males competition is not only acceptable but even a defining part of their masculinity. A father may take some pride in saying of his son, "He's a better man than I am"; but rare is the mother who says of her daughter, "She's a better woman than I am."

A difficult situation arises when the mother has encouraged her daughter's achievement strivings and independence because of what she believes to be her own failings and because she feels limited by her wife-mother roles. In this case, the daughter works hard in order to please the mother, to fulfill the mother's goals for her. As she comes close to meeting those goals, however, she usually realizes that while she was becoming an unusual woman, her mother was being a full-time wife and mother. She cannot know whether she could have come as far as she has if her mother had had her own vocation. Society has long subscribed to the notion that the best-adjusted, happiest children are raised by full-time mothers. The mother who wants to work elsewhere and does not, for whatever reason, usually needs to believe in that idea, and she communicates it to her daughter. Thus the successful daughter comes to feel that she owes success at least partly to her mother's "always being there when I came home from school." As it dawns on her that her mother would have enjoyed a career, she believes that her successes were attained at the expense of her mother's ambitions for herself. The result is a combination of guilt and anger toward the mother.

The daughter may also experience the same kind of confusion about the origins of her ambitions as she earlier experienced about her altruism and "goodness." Recognizing that her mother sacrificed ambitions for her sake, the daughter may begin to question how much her own current striving is simply to please her mother. As ambitiousness for women outside home and family becomes more common, daughters go through the same soul-searching as sons of ambitious parents: Is this for myself or for my parents? But again, with father and son there has been a difference. The son who surpasses his father's achievements is very unlikely to attribute his father's "failure" to the need to devote himself full-time to caretaking. He may feel some guilt and fear about outdoing his father, but these emotions are not products of the fathers' having denied themselves careers in order to raise their sons.

The daughter who senses that her mother feels competitive with her, or jealous of her accomplishments, often does one of two things or both at different times: (1) she reduces her efforts to achieve (or at least begins to conceal them from her mother), and (2) she creates an emotional distance from her mother. She may generally become more reserved around her mother, consciously decreasing her expectations for warmth and support from that source. Feeling envied by one's mother is a heavy burden; it intensifies any guilt the daughter has felt before about making her mother unhappy. Worse still, it reminds the daughter of her power to make her mother feel bad in the future; she senses that the choice is, horribly, hers in the trade-off of her mother's happiness for her own.

Horner's (1972) theory that women fear success because a successful woman may be rejected by society (or at least excluded from the traditionally sought-after roles of wife and mother) is given added force if we understand the emotional dynamics involved. Why do people come to fear the disapproval of society? One reason is that the rewards they want may be controlled by the sheer numbers of people represented by "society." But at a deep emotional level the fear of social disapproval begins in early childhood, with the child's first devastating experiences of parental anger. In *Sometimes I'm Jealous* (Watson et al., 1972), a book written for children by the Menninger Foundation, the child is reminded that angry parents "seemed very far away." This feeling of overwhelming loss and loneliness is at the bottom of the fear of social disapproval, and for a woman its most potent form often continues to be fear of the mother's disapproval.

If a daughter is the first woman in her family to choose an independent life, then she has no nearby model for such an endeavor. Even the son who outdoes his father is likely to have had a father who modeled achievement-striving behavior, if only because he was male. But the daughter who has a "full-time mother" has no such female model in the family. Insofar as parents are regarded as representative of what is "right," the daughter has to learn on her own how to want a career, independence, self-development, without feeling guilty or seeing herself as emotionally disturbed for having such goals.

Earlier, we discussed the myth that the daughter's marriage or giving birth brings mother and daughter closer together. In view of the increasing rate of separation and divorce, a word about the effect of the daughter's separation or divorce on her relationship with her mother is in order.

Separation and divorce fall under the rubric of "crises" in one's life. As with most crises, adults who were raised to believe in the notion that females are the sympathizers will expect their mothers to stand by their side through these difficult times. In Ingmar Bergman's film *Scenes from a Marriage,* the adult daughter asks why her divorce made her mother so angry: "After all, he left us for another woman. I'd have thought you'd have stood up for me." The mother replies that it was the young woman's father who was angry and that she herself felt they should not "interfere."

What happens most frequently takes one of two forms. In the first, the mother is even more threatened by her daughter's divorce than she was by the discord in the marriage itself. She is presented with the fact that unhappily married women have a choice; they need not suppress or learn to live with their unhappiness. If her own marriage has been unsatisfactory, she may find it more difficult to avoid taking some responsibility for creating a happier life for herself.

The other form of interaction that may occur is a real increase in the closeness and shared understanding between mother and daughter. A mother who observed her daughter's marital unhappiness and, for fear of "causing" her daughter to leave the marriage, hesitated to empathize and express her compassion may feel differently when faced with the divorce as a *fait accompli.* She may now allow herself to admit that marriage is not perfect, motherhood is not serene, and oppression of women is not fun for the victim. She may finally feel free to relax in her attempts to model that perfection of stereotype that was to persuade her daughter to join in perpetuation of the myth.

Many women now separating from their husbands say that for the first time in their lives they can talk fully and equally to their mothers. This may be due to the phenomena described above, but an additional element is often involved; that is, if the daughter requested the separation, or if she agreed that it was best, then she is likely to feel stronger than ever before. Many men and women going through separations and divorces find that they see themselves not only as separating from their spouses but also really for the first time, achieving true emotional separation from their parents, especially their mothers (Tessman, 1978). This increased strength and separateness makes it possible for daughters to cease their overprotective attitude toward their mothers and can pave the way for a fuller relationship between the two.

Still another phenomenon related to separation and divorce is that the daughter may be left feeling very lonely and, as an adult, may find herself able to recognize the need for "mothering" and nurturance, perhaps to request it from either parent or both for the first time in her life.

Another feature of the adult daughter's relationship with her mother concerns the mother's aging. A great deal of emotion can arise at the intersection of two issues in particular: the mother's aging and the daughter's decisions about reproduction. One consequence of a daughter's giving birth is that her mother thereby becomes a grandmother. As Mead observes in her autobiographical *Blackberry Winter* (1972), by the act of another something major happened in her life. The independent decision and action of her daughter and someone else resulted in the passing on of her own genes; a step had been taken toward perpetuation of some part of her. In this way, grandmotherhood can produce a sense of shared participation in the future by adult daughter and mother.

Continuing this theme, however, the potential for the daughter's sense of guilt is great. Many parents believe their children are their immortality; for women in particular, the fact that most of their value has come from child-rearing makes continuation of their genetic line especially important, for it is in some real sense a continuation (and even a justification) of their own lives. Therefore, a daughter who chooses not to bear children may feel a deep sense of guilt about interrupting the chain and, some believe, implicitly questioning the value of their mother's work of mothering. On a different level, women who feel useless when their children are grown often await (or even try to hasten) the birth of a grandchild, to allow them to resume mothering. A daughter who chooses not to reproduce, or who gives birth but limits the amount of mothering she hands over to her own mother, may therefore feel guilty of depriving the grandmother of a chance to play out her limited self-definition.

The other side of the daughter's capacity to pass on her mother's genes concerns the socially instilled fear of aging; becoming a grandmother is often accompanied by a sense of horror and dread. Our grandparents were, for most of us, the most salient and closest "old" people we knew as children. Many children first learn the word "old" in regard to their grandparents. Then, abruptly, with those memories in store, one is a grandmother; one has become old. Women's fear and anger about this is likely to be directed at the daughter, who is responsible for their unwanted status and who, this time, is the mirror.

CHAPTER 5

Related Issues

The formulations presented in this book may provide a basis for explaining some other characteristics of female psychological development. The suggestions in this chapter are intended to be reasonable hypotheses with heuristic aims, in need of extensive further exploration. We offer them because the issues they involve are crucial for the development of girls into women. About some of them, little has been written beyond asserting and reasserting conventional assumptions, e.g., that for a woman emotional involvement is more important in a sexual interaction than it is for a man. We do not know how much the truth varies from the stereotypes, and it is too complex and important a question to try to answer through questionnaire studies. But our clinical position has made it possible to observe and explore cases to which the conventional notion has applied. Perhaps as important as finding out the accuracy of any stereotype is exploring why people who do fit the stereotype have developed in that way. Finding such reasons is a first step toward expanding the possibilities for psychological and psychosexual development of women and of men.

Women's Need for Emotional Involvement in Sexual Interaction

One often hears that emotional involvement (being in love) with the sexual partner is more important to women than to men. Although it is now becoming clear that this is not always or inevitably true, I shall suggest two causative factors.

First of all, there are women's basic roles (Ayim, 1977): those of wife and mother, which for our purposes can be paired under the term "nurturer," and that of "bait," or object of decoration and sex. A woman who wanted to play out the sex-object role might measure her success by the degree of pleasure she gave her male partner. But this has been complicated by women's ambivalence about their own sexuality. Women's own enjoyment was both pleasurable and guilt-inducing, because they were supposed to be concerned more about the man's pleasure than their own. Women often learn that sex is to be endured for the man's sake. In this way, their "bait" role ultimately boils down to the nurturant, supportive role: Do what pleases the male, what makes him feel good and manly. In keeping with this same precept, as women's own sexual enjoyment has come to be considered acceptable, women have often continued to adapt their sexual experiences to the nurturant role, this time by pretending sexual enjoyment so the man would think he was a successful lover.

A sex object is something that, ultimately, one *is*. But being a nurturer is something one can *do;* one can always keep working to improve in the role. One of the few ways women have been able to feel they had some control over the people in their lives has been to aim to win security and protection, sometimes paired with and sometimes misnamed "love," in return for their sexual partnership. The wish has taken the form of "If I take good enough care of him, give him what he wants and needs, anticipate his desires both sexually and otherwise, then he will love or at least marry me." Thus the sexual sphere became a path to economic security, social acceptability and sometimes even emotional security. Its function was no different from that of cooking or having the man's slippers and martini ready when he stepped in the door after work. Sex, like everything else, was a route along which woman could offer her most valuable currency: her willingness to meet the man's needs, build up his ego, nurture him.

With this set of expectations and wishes, a woman could not bear the thought of a man taking her to bed and thinking nothing of her. This would mean ignoring the aspect of her that she could use, through her own effort, to maintain their relationship: nurturance. She could gauge for herself the extent to which she nurtured her man—preparing his meals, entertaining him and waiting on him— much better than she could know whether he obtained sexual pleasure anywhere else. What reassured her about continuity as his sexual partner was his need for her nurturance during the times in between their sexual encounters. This is one reason for jealousy of the female secretaries who bring coffee to the husbands, tidy their desks, order their lunches sent up, even choose birthday presents for the wife. Women have used a man's need for care and help as a sign that their relationship will continue, a sign that the sphere in which sheer effort can determine success—the nurturant role—remains available to them.

Rotkin (1972) considers a related point, the fact that women are socialized "to be content with the nonphysical rewards of intercourse" and to bear with the lack of physical rewards. She suggests that it is partially socialization that leads women to demand more "commitment" and "communication" from sexual contact than men generally do. She further proposes that emotional and nonphysical satisfactions have become to a large extent substitutions for physical, sexual satisfaction.

A second factor that may make it more likely for women to desire emotional involvement in a sexual relationship concerns their early relationships with their parents. As Freud (1905, 1932) describes these relationships, a boy tends to have important interactions with both parents by the time he is in his early childhood years while a girl tends to remain more exclusively attached to her mother. The reader will recall that this is because in our society the mother tends to be the primary love object, or source of both physical and emotional care, for children of both sexes. Then, when the process of identification begins, the boy takes his father as a model while to the girl her mother is a model in addition to the primary love object. This means that boys may be encouraged earlier in life both to withdraw some of their emotional investment in the object of their earliest physical and emotional closeness and to learn to form relationships of at least two kinds. Their relationship with their father has rewards that do not become confused with the giving or receiving of nurturance. At the risk of oversimplifying, it seems reasonable to assume, then, that the girl has a more restricted experience of relationships and that she spends a longer time primarily involved in her single, early relationship with her mother. One would predict that she would find it difficult to feel fulfilled by a relationship in which the physical and emotional aspects were not combined.

Infantilizing of Women

Many writers have said that men treat women as children in order to make themselves feel superior and in control. Women have often encouraged their men to treat them this way, and one of the reasons is that it is consistent with the female's obligation never to be threatening to the male by seeming stronger or more capable. But the nurturant role she is supposed to play is potentially extremely powerful; people who meet all our needs in fact have tremendous power over us, for what would we do if they stopped meeting our needs?

To avoid seeming too strong while being nurturers, women have often resorted to baby talk, playing dumb, meeting the husband's needs as a servant rather than as a strong mother would. Behaving in an infantile manner while meeting the husband's various needs is the pattern of the American female sex object: a very seductive woman's body topped by a baby-powder-pure, innocent, wide-eyed face—clean, well-scrubbed, well-groomed. Nothing is out of place, nothing out of control, nothing abandoned about her expression.

Playing such a childish role serves another purpose for women. It is the other side of their more customary role. When one tires of taking care of other people, the only two alternatives are being taken care of or being treated as an equal. The latter can sometimes include one party meeting some of the other person's needs, but few people are really comfortable with the idea of living with an equal. People are used to relationships in which the power balance is clear-cut. Men used to being nurtured by their wives, having their whims catered to and their idiosyncrasies or even their cruelties overlooked, are often frightened if their wives behave as equals, with needs as strong as their own. The woman's anger is expressed as a smile through clenched teeth; her sexual desire, through fluttering eyelids; her delight and joy, as "Oh, goody!" If she tries more adult forms of expression, she may risk scaring her husband so that he feels unable or unwilling to meet her needs.

Yet another factor contributes to the infantalizing of women. Both sons and daughters, because of the close relationship with their mother in infancy, associate infancy with the mother. This includes the state of infancy, the way people talk to infants, the sense of total security and protectedness, the absence of both gross motor activity and complex intellectual pursuit. The continued association of the mother with these characteristics is further facilitated by the continued presence in the home of the mother and not of the father, and by the mother's continuing responsibility for the rearing of the children as they grow older. In addition, the father is associated with other, more active pursuits that are appropriate for older children. It is not at all uncommon to hear a father acknowledge that he finally began to feel comfortable with his children when they "became people," that is, when they began to speak in sentences. It is less usual to hear a woman say this, which may indicate a difference in attitude, or in willingness to acknowledge comfort or discomfort with offspring of various developmental stages. Thus both the girl and the boy learn that what they received from the mother was what they desired as infants. The mother may tend to arouse the wish to be taken care of and the fear of slipping back into that early, protected but infantilizing type of relationship, the attitude "I don't want to get near it because I'm afraid I would never want to leave again."

As boys grow older and begin to identify with their fathers, they become more adult human males. As girls grow older and identify with their mothers, however, two things happen. On the one hand, their activities often take the form of nurturant behavior, which thrusts them from the infant's nurtured role into the role of provider of nurturance; from the latter position, the former can look temptingly attractive. On the other hand, as noted, much of the facade that women learn to create for themselves, in order to appear attractive and unthreatening to men, involves playing the role of a helpless infant. They have little opportunity to behave as mature but not caretaking adults. As Broverman and her co-investigators (1970) discovered, people use the same adjectives to describe a "healthy adult human being" and a "healthy male," but use many opposite adjectives to describe a "healthy female." By comparison, healthy females are supposed to be more submissive, less independent, less adventurous, more easily influenced, less aggressive and competitive, more emotional and more concerned about their appearance.

This suggests that the mothers who are raising such "healthy females" provide little opportunity, and instill little capacity in them, for behaving like their adult male contemporaries. Thus the daughters learn: "What my mother gave me is what an infant wants, and she cannot give me what a strong, self-respecting older person wants." Furthermore, it is largely for the benefit of the nearby males that the daughter fails to develop or, in some cases, conceals her strengths and her autonomy. Therefore, she is left with little chance to practice being an autonomous adult. She is usually either nurturer or infant.

Why Do Women Become Heterosexual?

In theory, heterosexuality, bisexuality and homosexuality might coexist, each present in some members of the species, but some heterosexuality is necessary to preserve the species. The physiological changes in adolescence help many people along the path to a heterosexual orientation.

If one had to decide whether, within a species, pairs of individuals should be similar or different, in order to maximize survival value one would choose that they be different. Division of labor and maintenance of a "gene pool" of the widest possible range of behavior would be the reasons for this choice. The need to keep the gene pool large and varied has been suggested as one of the most compelling explanations for the origin of prohibitions against incest and marriage within the family: the greatest possible mixture of the population allows for the widest variety and, therefore, the greatest chances for adaptability of the species. Now, since two women together cannot reproduce, this argument does not immediately apply to the question of heterosexuality or homosexuality. Only heterosexual couples can reproduce and change the gene pool in any direct way. If there is some innate tendency toward the attraction of different individuals, however, this would tend to encourage heterosexual rather than homosexual pairs. In addition, the more exclusively homosexual pairs are formed, the more the gene pool is restricted by the removal of the genes of both members of these pairs from the reproductive pool. Considering that a girl's closest relationship tends to be with her mother, that the mother is available to her more of the time and is more emotionally accessible than the father, and that the daughter often finds herself in the same predicaments as the mother, one might wonder how and why females ever become psychologically heterosexual.

Typically, heterosexuality is regarded as the norm and homosexuality as a deviation, and then attempts are made to explain the deviation. Some widely accepted theories describe homosexuality, in both females and males, as an "arrest in development"; that is, people are assumed to be homosexual because, for a variety of reasons, they have not yet gone beyond that stage to the "higher" or at least later stage of heterosexuality. Sullivan (1953) has pointed out the importance of the "chum" stage in the development of a person's strength and self-confidence. The chum, according to Sullivan, is a same-sex peer outside the person's family with whom secrets may be shared and comparisons made of feelings, wishes and thoughts, as well as bodies. These are an important part of individuals' attempts to learn what is usual and what is strange about themselves. Learning that a chum sometimes has similar thoughts, for example, makes one feel less isolated, less "weird," less inadequate.

Taking this into account, there might be two categories of reasons for not moving into a heterosexual relationship: (1) aspects of heterosexuality might be distasteful, frightening or disconcerting to the individual, and (2) the individual might not have gained sufficient strength and self-confidence from the chum stage because of the lack of a chum or preexisting difficulties that make it impossible to benefit sufficiently from a chum. Aspects included in the first category would be the fear of pregnancy, observations of males treating females as sex objects or otherwise inferior beings, or the preference for a style of interaction generally considered inappropriate (and, therefore, having become rare) for men, such as expression of tender feelings. Included in the second category would be individuals who consider themselves insufficiently attractive to the other sex, who believe they have no idea what members of the other sex find attractive or interesting, or who are so generally insecure that they even have trouble forming genuinely close relationships with members of the same sex.*

---

*Dinnerstein (1977) has suggested that women cannot relax and enjoy sex with men because their partners' gender is different from that of their first love: the mother. Such a view would make it still more difficult to explain how women ever become heterosexual. But it seems more likely that many of women's anxieties about heterosexual sex result from having experienced men as initiators, directors and controllers of power in both sexual and nonsexual areas of personal and public life. Therefore, a heterosexual encounter is often yet another situation in which a woman feels powerless.

But what factors might favor the passing of a girl or woman into heterosexuality? A daughter's sense of being intruded upon, of being too much understood by her mother, may help turn her toward heterosexuality. She may believe that a male is more likely to appreciate her good characteristics, probably because they are so different from his own. She may feel he is less likely to consider her weaknesses to be drawbacks, because he does not quite understand them. Or she may believe that both she and the male can defuse the "badness" of her drawbacks by attributing them to her gender: "Oh, women are just *like* that."

For some women the most attractive aspect of heterosexuality is that it allows them to dissociate themselves from a group regarded as inferior and to become instead associated with their men: "I am *Mrs. John Smith.*"

The process of establishing independence and identity may make heterosexuality seem attractive. In this process, one needs to learn by comparison with similar (e.g., same-sex) individuals but also by contrast (or even comparison of similarities) with individuals who belong to other categories (e.g., members of the opposite sex). People learn who they are by observing not only who is similar but also who looks and behaves differently: these differences lead to taking note of one's own position on various continua of body, behavior, emotion and belief. Furthermore, when people see similarities between themselves and others who are in some way very different (with respect to gender, for example), they acquire some insight into the origins of various components of themselves and the extent to which they may be more flexible. One may turn to the other sex not only because of biological-sexual impetus but also as a part of a more complex cognitive and emotional process of self-definition and self-exploration.

A woman may find greater security in being with other women; having the same kind of body and having been raised with similar sex-role expectations, they know what she wants almost before she knows it herself. Some women find they either do not need that security or cannot withstand the vulnerability involved in being an "open book" to their partner. Still others find it more comforting or interesting to explore the differences between self and partner when the two are apparently similar because of belonging to the same gender category. (Kate Millett's *Sita*, 1977, explores this last type of relationship.) This discussion is not meant to ignore the fact that some women in heterosexual relationships are easily understood by their partners, or that some women in homosexual relationships are easily understood by their partners, or that some women in homosexual relationships are not well understood. These outcomes depend on the sum of life experiences, and I am here indicating some important tributaries.

Women's Sense of Justice

Two popular notions about women seem to contradict each other. One is that women are both more compassionate and more religious than men. The other, an ancient idea more recently delineated in psychoanalytic terms by Freud (1964), is that men's sense of justice is superior to women's. On the surface, these two statements may appear to be compatible: compassion and religion would involve emotions whereas a sense of justice would require the use of logic and an analytic approach, and the stereotypic description of women is emotional and of men is logical and rational. Before further exploring these ideas, it will be helpful to examine Freud's theory that castration anxiety is the source of the alleged sex difference in the sense of justice.

According to Freud (1964), boys and girls each wish to possess the opposite-sex parent, and both suppress the wish because they fear they will be punished by, and lose the love of, the same-sex parent. Freud suggests that boys have more reason to be afraid, because only they can be punished by castration. One means of evading the wrath of the same-sex parent is to identify with that parent, adopting that parent's values (i.e., "internalizing" the values, or developing a superego or conscience). This, Freud says, is how the standards of society are transmitted from one generation to the next, and males are the more important transmitters since their fear of castration provides the motivation and force for the internalizing of standards.

Our discussion in previous chapters would suggest a different outcome. One might expect girls to have strong superegos because of the combination of two tasks that they must negotiate: (1) suppressing their own wish for nurturance in order to nurture others and (2) rechanneling the libidinal energy bound up in their attachment to the mother so they do not become homosexual.

What is justice, and how does it differ from the allegedly "feminine" compassion? Justice involves a weighing of principles that conflict, usually in a manner that has practical consequences. In criminal law, it may be the freedom of two people that conflicts: one wishes to stretch freedom of action to the point of murder, and the other wishes to continue to live. In civil law, a conflict may occur regarding the rights of two people to own the same thing: both may have paid for the same piece of land, believing they were contracting with its rightful owner; in fact, however, only one dealt with the owner, while the other dealt with an impostor. Compassion involves a feeling of sympathy with, and understanding of, another person's feelings. One may have more or less compassion for murderer and victim, or for both parties in a civil suit; but justice demands that the rights or freedoms of one party be given precedence over those of the other. A choice, a decision must be made. One could hardly believe, however, that the business or manual labor experiences to which adult males are exposed would better fit them for such decision-making than the constant decisions and choices that mothers, day-care workers, baby-sitters and female teachers must make in the daily disputes among children in their care. If women are less capable, then it would indeed be alarming that society grants them the job of teaching and raising children.

If boys and girls in the beginning and middle phases of superego development cannot yet comprehend important principles of justice, and if the traditionally different experiences of males and females in adulthood do not provide better training for men, how can one justify the assumption that men have a greater sense of justice?

The training of females to carry out the nurturer's role aims to make them more compassionate, more sensitive to the feelings of others; indeed, their whole sense of identity may depend on this. Compassion is an essential ingredient of a sense of justice, for in weighing two conflicting principles it is often essential to understand the feelings and intentions of the two parties. Yet justice requires more than compassion. One must also be able to limit one's own involvement in the feelings of others in order to make a choice that will disappoint at least one of the parties involved. The teaching of males to suppress their feelings and base their actions on reason might well make it easier for men to make decisions on issues of justice, but one would be concerned about their capacity for considering the effects of their decisions on the people involved.

In addition, laws and rules of justice vary from one society to another. An important source of these principles in our society has been humane considerations, feelings of compassion, and strictures of religion. Most laws and rules of justice are applications of such considerations to technical or complex situations. Thus the distinction between compassion and a sense of justice is by no means clear-cut, and the assertion that one sex outranks the other in one of these areas becomes questionable.

CHAPTER 6

Lowering the Barriers

How do mothers,
unloved, love
their children?
the wonder is that
we do, we
do not destroy
we cry out in terror
we love
our little girls
who must have a
better life . . .

—Alta, "Placenta Previa," in *Momma:*
A Start on All the Untold Stories (1974)

The barriers between women present a picture that is neither entirely negative in its implications nor without hope for change. The
multiple connections between mother and daughter provide a foundation for a potentially close, positive relationship. But the lack of
continuity in the feminist movement during this century reflects the
fact that mothers and daughters, women and other women, have
not often banded together to share support, warmth and the
strength that can be channeled into improving their lot.

In a sexist society, women's tendency to ally themselves with
other women continues to be (a) temporary, until a man comes
along, and/or (b) as members of an oppressed class and therefore
united by their difference from men (and, at the extreme, against
men themselves). The breakdown of sexism would allow women to
form allegiances and friendships with other women because of the
similarities as well as the differences in their experiences, shared
goals, needs for mutual support; these could be friendships of
choice rather than necessity, friendships and loyalties that could

endure regardless of the vicissitudes of their relationships with men. They could concentrate on their functions as an in-group rather than as a group that sets up out-groups; they could be more *for* themselves and each other than against any other individual, group or movement.

The changes that people can make in their relationships are difficult to discuss outside the context of the present nature of society and the possibilities for social change. This is particularly the case when the issue is women's relationships with each other, because standards of sex-appropriate behavior have recently undergone some changes, and many more remain to be improved.

What can be done to lower the barriers between women? It is essential to understand that social change can have profound effects on how individuals relate to each other emotionally and psychologically. Griffin (1977) pointed out that the generally acknowledged experts in child-rearing operate on the assumption that this function belongs to the mother. She notes that these experts are "forever concerned with damages to children in this closed system" but that the

> negligences, rages, injustices of the mother are never explained. In their accounts it is as if the mother simply lacked skill or human understanding. Dr. Ginott suggests that a mother who vented her rage at her son should have 'confined herself to one sentence. . . .' I read the word 'confined' and I think—anger confined, sexuality confined, movement confined, thoughts confined. And that in Dr. Ginott's columns only the children have names. (p. 100)

Griffin asks: "And why is it in the case of women that we always blame the individual and not the social structure. That we see failure in discrete lives and do not question 'the way things are.' " (p. 100)

To begin with, both parents can teach the daughter that her worth comes from many sources; it should not depend disproportionately on her ability to nurture others. Parents can instead teach her how to take responsibility for herself and how to behave with humanity toward others.

In his poem "A Prayer for My Daughter" (1921/1962), Yeats' ideal for his daughter is self-defined, not dependent on meeting the needs of others. He realized that to define oneself as meeter of the needs of others means that only other people can decide whether one has succeeded. This leads to dependent, frightened women. His hope was that his daughter's soul would learn "at last that it is self-delighting,/self-appeasing, self-affrighting,/And that its own sweet will is Heaven's will . . .''

Minimizing the sex differences in child-rearing would mean neither parent would have to set more rigid limits on the behavior of daughters as compared to that of sons. Furthermore, making the nurturant role less exclusively female, and opening all roles to both sexes, would mean no one could assume that girls should automatically be shaped to fit the nurturing role.

Substantial differences in the raising of male and female children persist, but there are signs that they are decreasing. One is the fact that there is now more questioning of the consequences of these differences than at any time since the 1920's. In addition, changes in dress reflect a belief that girls and women have the right to put their comfort ahead of a doll-like appearance.

A significant change of practice that indicates changes in attitudes is the decreasing tendency of women to take their husbands' last names or to pass them on to their children. (This is reflected in the daily records of even small-town newspapers. Compared to the figures of five years ago, the number of divorcing women who are requesting restoration of their maiden names is increasing; they no longer cling to the name of their former mate as a sign of their identity.) As long as only sons can carry on the family name, they will be a source of greater pride than daughters. In one case, an exquisitely beautiful girl in her early teens, beginning with the belief that only her brother would carry on the family name, interpreted every difference in her parents' treatment of herself and her brother in that light. There was serious emotional disturbance in her make-up, but the point is made that this is not a neutral practice.

Along with the breakdown of sex-role stereotyping, society's regard for women is improving. This is a step toward ensuring that parents will be as pleased by the birth of a daughter as by that of a son. Pride in a daughter from the moment of birth (or even anticipatory pride beforehand) sets the stage for encouraging her toward the same goals as a son for happiness, self-actualization and success. This is important to the mother of a new baby in at least three ways: first, for a sense of her own worth and pleasure in giving birth to a child of either sex; second, for the freedom from fear of her husband's disappointment, disparagement of her and the girl child, and even anger; and third, for the freedom from fear of the disparagement of the rest of society (often including her own parents) if she bears a daughter.

Popular psychological literature is helping people to realize that physical expressions of affection belong on a continuum that includes but by no means necessarily leads to overt, unrestrained sexual contact. Thus mothers may learn that holding and loving their daughters will not cause them to become homosexual or adversely affect sexual development. What such behavior can do is help daughters feel loved and cared for, as it frees mothers to express love as openly for their daughters as for their sons.

There are two general rules that a mother can follow in order to minimize many of the problems in the mother-daughter relationship. One is to make clear her own dilemmas. Rather than encouraging a picture of herself as an "ideal" mother who copes with her tasks selflessly and serenely, she can explain to her daughter some of the conflicts, ambivalence and exhaustion she feels. Good parenting includes describing and explaining reality and presenting alternative points of view and ways to cope. Mothers who do not do so will continue to lay the foundations for their daughters' sense of inadequacy when they become wives and mothers. The blurring of sex roles is well on its way, but neither the current rules nor the ultimate outcomes are by any means clear. The daughter whose mother is a source of strength, an ally with whom she can discuss alternatives and uncertainties without fearing either her mother's perfection or her mother's collapse, can find in her a model of strength and independence. Through her mother's example, she may find her own strength and capacity for warmth.

A specific case in which mothers can help their daughters concerns the "unfeminine" emotion of anger. Because anger is a natural human emotion but has been labeled unfeminine, women have felt that their anger proved they were bad people (deSousa, 1978). Mothers can teach their daughters by example that anger is human, does not make people less than human if properly directed. Rich (1976) understands how germane to the daughter's learning to deal with her own anger is the mother's way of dealing with anger herself: "A woman who has used her anger creatively will not seek to suppress anger in her daughter in fear that it could become, merely, suicidal." (p. 245) Indeed, this is where girls' and women's guilt when they feel angry has tended to lead them. Once they brand their anger as a sign of "bitchiness" (deSousa, 1978), they tend to turn that anger toward themselves. Research indicates that disturbed or even so-called "antisocial" or delinquent females tend to have more self-punishing or escapist symptoms than boys, who are more likely to act out their aggression on things or other people (for example, see Caplan et al., 1979).

The sharing of experiences that a mother can promote between herself and her daughter can also occur with beneficial effects between adult women. Women's groups that allow their members to share rage and frustration, joy, and dilemma or conflict in the roles of woman, wife and mother can do much to reduce each member's isolation from the others and from a sense of what is reasonable for human beings who are trying to define and live out these roles.

Another general rule for mothers is to become as strong and self-sufficient as possible. They must be able to confront, on their own, society's disapproval if they do not "shape" their daughters to the usual patterns. A mother who does not feel embarrassed or inadequate when asked whether her daughter is *still* unmarried does her daughter a great service. A mother who does not feel it is her own triumph when her daughter becomes engaged is keeping her needs separate from her daughter's; this allows the daughter the freedom of real choice.

Rich (1976) has written: "As daughters we need mothers who want their own freedom and ours." (p. 247) Daughters who have weak mothers often have assumed the nurturant role toward the mother; in this case, the daughter's apparent or real strength is based on the fear that, were it not for her caretaking, the mother might "disintegrate" (go crazy, leave the family or become angry, depending upon the family's concerns).

Under these circumstances, mothers can help both themselves and their daughters by investing some time and energy outside the family. The family then learns that the mother's life does not depend upon the family alone, and the daughter in particular learns that she is not responsible for her mother's emotional state.

It is also helpful if fathers do not invest too much of their energy in producing a socially approved daughter, though there is less danger of such an overinvestment on their part. The father's vocation, together with his hobbies, is considered a crucial part of his life; it shapes his reputation at least as much as the personal successes of his wife and children. But even the mother who works outside the home knows that her reputation depends largely on her children's conduct and achievements. What is more, her daughter knows this. Therefore, it becomes extremely important for mothers and fathers to show that they will not fall apart or be ashamed if their daughters deviate from approved paths, wholeheartedly pursue careers, decide not to marry or have children, have "illegitimate" pregnancies, get divorced or become homosexual. This relieves the daughters of a burden of guilt that is potentially devastating and can drive them to suicide, unhappy marriages, and unwanted births and abortions.

There is a growing trend toward a real sharing of child-rearing tasks between mothers and fathers, with work arrangements that make this possible. One can foresee that this major social change would have valuable consequences for the issues that have been the focus of this book. Even before this change pervades society, a daughter who sees it in her own parents can benefit substantially. Watching her father take an equal share in raising children, she will learn that not all the responsibility for child care and the child's "acceptability" to society is up to the mother. She is less likely to assume that her own worth will come, in toto, from her success as a raiser of children. She will not have as a model a mother whose self-esteem comes entirely from such a role.

The father can participate in child-rearing throughout the child's life. Yet even the way the father treats his wife during pregnancy, his attitude toward her being pregnant, can lay the foundations for a sharing of experience between husband and wife that moves naturally into shared child-rearing. The fatigue and physical disabilities that often accompany pregnancy have sometimes been interpreted by psychotherapists as expressions of the woman's ambivalence about being pregnant, but it is known that the hormonal changes during pregnancy often cause these debilitating effects; this is also true for hormonal changes that take place soon after delivery and with the beginning, continuation and cessation of nursing.

One might speculate that the real physical disabilities of this period have important value for the survival of the species: because the woman is less able to care for herself (and later for the infant), preservation of the species requires that other adults participate in the care of the pregnant woman and then of the infant. — The interpersonal theory of personality (Leary, 1957), which holds that passive and submissive behavior in humans tends to elicit dominant and caretaking behavior in other people, has important implications for the father's parenting role. The pregnant woman's need of care and nurturance tends to evoke such behavior in at least one other adult, so that there would now be at least two adults to protect and care for the body that is incubating the infant and eventually for the infant itself. This has clear survival value. In addition, because humans are social and emotional rather than just behavioral creatures, there is the potential for creating a closer bond *between the caretakers* (e.g., mother and father) and *between the non-mother caretaker* (e.g., father) *and the baby.*

In this light, we understand (1) that the recent emphasis on parents' sharing of the childbirth experience should naturally be extended to a sharing of the entire pregnancy, and (2) that the idea of a child's biological mother being the best suited or the only appropriate person to provide total care to her infant appears incorrect.

Men's potential for warm parenting has become especially clear recently as a result of the rising divorce rate, which often has meant that fathers are left alone with their children, at least on visiting days. Griffin (1977) writes: "The link between child and parent is not an irreversible fate of biology. After the divorce, my daughter and her father spend long hours alone together. They become close. He develops subtle understandings. He mothers." (p. 102)

Shared child-rearing would also help to demythologize motherhood by reducing the isolation of mothers from other people who are raising children. A mother who felt insecure about or exhausted by her parenting duties could turn to her husband for a sharing of these frustrations. This is the kind of checking and sharing that may have taken place when extended families were the norm. It is another way to provide mothers the support they need in order to be strong for their daughters.

Still another problem that would be helped by equal sharing of parenting between mothers and fathers is the daughter's perception of her mother as intrusive (see Chapter IV). A daughter's sense of intrusiveness comes partly from her excessive dependence on the mother as a source of support and information. For the teenager, this becomes threatening every time her need for separateness arises; a hothouse atmosphere develops, and she must leave the family to escape being enveloped by the only close relationship with an adult that she can maintain there. There are no alternatives within the family; there are no ways to explore other facets of herself, for she is limited to those that her mother notices, allows, can encourage or understand. The presence of two supportive, emotionally accessible parents (or other adults) within the family gives the daughter more freedom within her own home, more opportunity for variety and self-exploration. Less dependent on her mother, she has less reason to fear her mother's understanding and to experience it as intrusive.

As males become freer to show their feelings and to share in the child-raising, they also will become demythologized. Wives and children will observe that, upon assuming half the caretaking responsibilities, men will find it no easier to control their fears, frustrations and needs than women have been.

The father's equal share in child-rearing can also alleviate the disturbing consequences of the fear of homosexuality inherent in the mother-daughter relationship. Having a close, emotional and expressive relationship with her father decreases the intensity and exclusivity of the daughter's relationship with her heretofore primary love object, her mother. At a different level, because the daughter can begin to develop a close, emotional relationship with a parent of each sex, the fear that the child will be able to form relationships only with other females loses much of its foundation. The mother can observe that the warmth and physical affection she offers do not make her daughter receptive to such things only from an adult who is female.

Shared child-rearing and the breakdown of sex-role stereotypes will help both mother and daughter to have relationships with men that are freer from the fear that men will find their concerns and feelings mysterious, trivial or irrelevant. It will become easier to regard men as other than objects of envy or as helpless children. Penis pity is one feeling based on physical fact and certain normal attitudes of human development that illustrates ways in which women can share feelings among themselves that are not based on the assumption of male superiority. One might feel the same relief about not having a vulnerable organ as when it is "the other guy" who slips and falls: "I'm glad it wasn't me, but I can empathize with the person it happened to." This is just one example of the concerns that most men experience but from which women have been barred from empathizing with, having been taught to consider themselves inferior to anything male. Compassion for the concerns of an equal is more consistent with the humane ideal than is fear or envy. Women can share a compassion for men, united in their freedom both from concerns that men may inevitably have (because of physical differences) and from those that they need not always bear alone (such as "being the breadwinner"). Women may also come closer to men through the greater understanding of men's real problems, instead of helping to support the male myths (e.g., that men do not need to talk about their feelings, that they never enjoy a sexually passive role).

On an individual basis, one woman to another, attempts can be made to go beyond myth and tradition. Women can purge their relationships with other women of the myth that they must be nurturant, long-suffering, self-denying, never angry in their own defense. They can refuse to put their relationships with men ahead of their relationships with each other. (Alcott, 1978, illustrates how, once rivalry for a man is removed, intense hostility between two women can give way to a close and warm alliance.) The fifteen-year-old girl who cancels a date with a girlfriend in order to see a boy will have trouble, when she becomes a mother, not treating her daughter as a poor substitute for male company. A married woman, or a woman who is clearly attached to a man, can refuse to encourage the attitude that her first loyalty is to her husband, no matter what. Such an attitude is considered reprehensible, for example, when a lieutenant breaks the "rules" of war and shoots civilians on the orders of a superior, but women have been encouraged to support their husbands, right or wrong. In some cases, depending on circumstances, it is a justifiable attitude to put first a relationship to which one has made a long-term commitment. But a woman who supports her husband in immoral, unprincipled behavior undermines her own self-respect in order to protect her physical self economically and to avoid the possibility of facing life without the support of a man, perhaps even alone. She undermines not only her self-respect, but also her other potential source of emotional support, fun and friendship, if she disregards women friends in order to protect her husband's reprehensible behavior or to cater to his whims when they are childish or self-centered.

Greer's (1970) comments on the mythology of the first kiss and on that of marriage are relevant here. These myths, she points out, were useful when women needed men to give them economic security and social acceptability. They were also necessary to attract a woman to a situation in which she could permanently do what a woman does best: nurturing. As women discover wider possibilities for their lives, find they can support themselves economically and are strong enough not to marry or attach themselves to a man out of weakness and need, the usefulness of these myths decreases. Correspondingly, as people search for meaning and happiness in life, they often find it lies in two major areas: their self-actualization and their friendships. In this context, the potential for women's friendships with other women is further enhanced.

Griffin (1977) has written: "I remember my fury at the constrictions placed upon me as a child. I remember the look of innocence on my daughter's face. . . . And that when I realized I'd given birth to a girl my heart opened to myself and all the suffering of women seemed unreasonable to me." (p. 100) In the past, the pain of that opening and viewing has led many women to retreat to the traditional rules for raising and restricting daughters, and their retreat was encouraged by a society that refused to acknowledge its unfair treatment of women. But women's support of other women, and women's and men's growing acknowledgment of the past unfairness, gives new encouragement to the mothers of daughters. With such support, they can face the pain in their own past and shape something better for their children.

References

Alcott, Louisa May. *Behind a Mask* (M. Stern, ed.). Bantam Books, Toronto (1978).

Alta. Placenta previa, in *Momma: A Start on All the Untold Stories.* Times Change Press, Albion, Calif. (1974).

Ayim, Maryann. Inaloosiak's dilemma—every woman's heritage. Presented to Canadian Society of Women in Philosophy. Toronto (1977).

Bardwick, Judith M., and Douvan, Elizabeth. Ambivalence: the socialization of women, in *Woman in Sexist Society* (Vivan Gornick and Barbara K. Moran, eds.). Basic Books, New York (1971), pp. 225–41.

Belotti, Elena Gianini. *Little Girls.* Writers and Readers Publishing Cooperative, London (1975).

Bernard, Jessie. *The Future of Motherhood.* Dial Press, New York (1974).

Bowlby, John. *Attachment and Loss.* Vol. I: *Attachment.* Basic Books, New York (1969).

―――. Academic lecture at Clarke Institute of Psychiatry. Toronto (June 15, 1978).

Broverman, Inge K.; Broverman, Donald M.; Clarkson, Frank E.; Rosenkrantz, Paul S.; and Vogel, Susan R. Sex role stereotypes and clinical judgments of mental health. *Journal of Consulting and Clinical Psychology* 34 (1970), 1–7.

Caplan, Paula J. The role of classroom conduct in the promotion and retention of elementary school children. *Journal of Experimental Education* 41 (1973a), 8–11.

―――. Sex differences in antisocial behavior. Unpublished Ph.D. dissertation. Duke University (1973b).

―――. Sex differences in response to school failure. *Journal of Learning Disabilities* 7 (1974), 49–52.

―――. Sex differences in antisocial behavior: does research methodology produce or abolish them? *Human Development* 18 (1975), 444–60.

―――. Beyond the box score: A boundary condition for sex differences in aggression and achievement striving, in *Progress in Experimental Personality Research* (Vol. 9) (Brendan Maher, ed.). Academic Press, Inc., New York (1979).

―――. Awad, George; Wilks, Corinne; and White, Georgina. Sex differences in a family court clinic delinquent population. Presented to Canadian Psychological Association. (Quebec City, 1979).

Chesler, Phyllis. *Women and Madness.* Avon Books, New York (1973).

Claremont de Castillejo, Irene. *Knowing Woman.* Harper & Row, New York (1973).

Clark, Lorenne M. G. A Marxist-feminist critique of Marx and Engels; or, the consequences of seizing the reins in the household. Presented to Canadian Society of Women in Philosophy. Toronto (1978).

Coser, Lewis. *The Functions of Social Conflict.* Free Press, New York (1956).

de Beauvoir, Simone. *A Very Easy Death.* Penguin Books, Ltd., Harmonds-
worth, Middlesex, England (1969).
―――. *The Second Sex.* Vintage Books, New York (1974).
de Sousa, R. B. Self-deceptive emotions. *Journal of Philosophy* 75 (1978), 684–97.
Dinnerstein, Dorothy. *The Mermaid and the Minotaur.* Harper Colophon Books,
New York (1977).
Erikson, Erik H. Identity and the life cycle. Monograph, *Psychological Issues,*
Vol. I, No. 1. International Universities Press, New York (1959).
―――. *Identity, Youth, and Crisis.* W. W. Norton, New York (1968).
Frank, Anne. *The Diary of a Young Girl* (B. M. Mooyart-Doubleday, transl.).
Doubleday, Garden City, N.Y. (1952).
Freud, Sigmund. Three essays on a theory of sexuality (1905), in *The Standard
Edition of the Complete Psychological Works of Sigmund Freud,* Vol. VII
(James Strachey, transl.). Hogarth Press and Institute of Psycho-analysis, Lon-
don (1953).
―――. Mourning and melancholia (1917), in *The Standard Edition of the Com-
plete Psychological Works of Sigmund Freud,* Vol. XIV (James Strachey,
transl.). Hogarth Press and Institute of Psycho-analysis, London (1957).
―――. Civilization and its discontents (1930), in *The Standard Edition of the
Complete Psychological Works of Sigmund Freud,* Vol. XXI (James Strachey,
transl.). Hogarth Press and Institute of Psycho-analysis, London (1961a).
―――. Female sexuality (1931), in *The Standard Edition of the Complete Psy-
chological Works of Sigmund Freud,* Vol. XXI (James Strachey, transl.). Ho-
garth Press and Institute of Psycho-analysis, London (1961b).
―――. Introductory lectures on psychoanalysis (1915–1917), in *The Standard
Edition of the Complete Psychological Works of Sigmund Freud,* Vols. XV and
XVI (James Strachey, transl.). Hogarth Press and Institute of Psycho-analysis,
London (1961 and 1963).
―――. Negation (1925), in *The Standard Edition of the Complete Psychological
Works of Sigmund Freud,* Vol. XIX (James Strachey, transl.). Hogarth Press
and Institute of Psycho-analysis, London (1961c).
―――. Femininity (in New introductory lectures in psychoanalysis, 1932), in *The
Standard Edition of the Complete Psychological Works of Sigmund Freud,* Vol.
XXII (James Strachey, transl.). Hogarth Press and Institute of Psycho-analysis,
London (1964).
Friday, Nancy. *My Mother/My Self.* Delacorte Press, New York (1977).
Friedan, Betty. *The Feminine Mystique.* Dell, New York (1963).
Gadlin, Howard. Discussion in Symposium on Father-Daughter Incest. Presented
at American Psychological Association Convention. Toronto (1978).
Gilligan, Carol. Quoted in Our radically changing society: report on the precen-
tennial conference "perspectives on the patterns of an era," by Aida K. Press.
Radcliffe Quarterly (June 1978).
Gornick, Vivan, and Barbara K. Moran, eds. *Woman in Sexist Society.* Basic
Books, New York (1971).
Greer, Germaine. *The Female Eunuch.* Paladin, London (1970).

Griffin, Susan. Forum: on wanting to be the mother I wanted. *MS.* Vol. V, No. 7 (January 1977), 98–105.

Hammer, Signe. *Daughters and Mothers: Mothers and Daughters.* Signet, New York (1976).

Harding, M. Esther. *The Way of All Women.* Harper & Row, New York (1970).

Hite, Shere. *The Hite Report.* Dell, New York (1976).

Horner, Matina S. Toward an understanding of achievement-related conflicts in women. *Journal of Social Issues* 28 (1972), 157–75.

Horney, Karen. *New Ways in Psychoanalysis.* W. W. Norton, New York (1966).

Kaplan, Alexandra. Moderator's discussion in Symposium on Father-Daughter Incest. Presented to American Psychological Association. Toronto (1978).

Kennedy, Florynce. *Color Me Flo: My Hard Life and Good Times.* Prentice-Hall, Englewood Cliffs, N.J. (1976).

Klein, George S. Freud's two theories of sexuality, in *Clinical Cognitive Psychology: Models and Integrations* (L. Breger, ed.). Prentice-Hall, Englewood Cliffs, N.J. (1969), pp. 136–81.

Kohlberg, Lawrence, and Zigler, L. The impact of cognitive maturity on the development of sex-role attitudes in the years 4 to 8. *Genetic Psychological Monographs* 75 (1967), 89–165.

Kome, Penny. Woman's place. *Homemaker's* (June/July/August 1977), 72B–72H.

Lange, Lynda. Woman is not a rational animal: on Aristotle's biology of reproduction. Presented to Canadian Society of Women in Philosophy. Toronto (1977).

Laurence, Margaret. *The Diviners.* Bantam Books, Toronto (1976).

Leary, Timothy. *Interpersonal Diagnosis of Personality.* Ronald Press, New York (1957).

Lerner, Gerda. *The Female Experience: An American Documentary.* Bobbs-Merrill, Indianapolis (1977).

Lerner, Harriet. Sugar and spice . . . the taboos against female anger. *Menninger Perspective.* (Winter 1977), 5–11.

Lynn, David. *The Father: His Role in Child Development.* Brooks/Cole, Monterey, Calif. (1974).

Marshall, John. Quoted in The weaker sex? Hah! *Time* (June 26, 1978), 60.

McGinley, Phyllis. Girl's-eye view of relatives, in *Times Three.* Viking Press, New York (1960).

McGrady, Mike. Family banking. *New York* (June 12, 1972), 42.

Mead, Margaret. *Male and Female.* William Morrow, New York (1949).

———. *Blackberry Winter.* Simon & Schuster, New York (1972).

Means, Robert T., Jr. Letter to the editor. *Psychology Today* (November 1974), 14.

Miller, Casey, and Swift, Kate. *Words and Women.* Anchor Books, Garden City, N.Y. (1977).

Millett, Kate. *Sexual Politics.* Avon Books, New York (1969).

———. *Sita.* McGraw-Hill, New York (1977).

Neisser, Edith. *Mothers and Daughters.* Harper & Row, New York (1973).

Nietzsche, Friedrich. *The Portable Nietzsche* (Walter Kaufman, transl. and ed.). Viking Press, New York (1954).

Psychology Today. "Newsline" (August, 1974), 29.

Raphael, Betty-Jane. Mothers and daughters. *Ladies' Home Journal* (September 1978).

Reeves, Nancy. *Womankind: Beyond the Stereotype.* Aldine, Atherton, Chicago (1971).

Rich, Adrienne. *Of Woman Born.* W. W. Norton, New York (1976).

Rotkin, Karen. The phallacy of our sexual norm. *RT: A Journal of Radical Therapy* (formerly *Rough Times, Radical Therapist*), Vol. 3, No. 1 (September 1972).

Rowbotham, Sheila. *Woman's Consciousness, Man's World.* Penguin Books, Ltd., Harmondsworth, Middlesex, England (1973).

Ryan, Mary P. *Womanhood in America: From Colonial Times to the Present.* New Viewpoints, New York (1975).

Sanger, Sirgay. Personal communication (February 1979).

Sexton, Anne. Housewife, in *All My Pretty Ones.* Riverside Press, Cambridge, Mass. (1961), p. 48.

Sheehy, Gail. *Passages.* Bantam Books, New York (1976).

Shields, Carol. *Small Ceremonies.* Totem, Toronto (1976).

Sigourney, Lydia Howard. *Letters to Mothers.* Harper and Brothers, New York (1845).

Smith, Liz. *The Mother Book.* Doubleday, Garden City, N.Y. (1978).

Smith, Selwyn. *The Battered Child Syndrome.* Butterworths, London (1975).

Sullivan, Harry Stack. *The Interpersonal Theory of Psychiatry.* W. W. Norton, New York (1953).

Tessman, Lora Heims. *Children of Parting Parents.* Jason Aronson, New York (1978).

Totah, Norma. Personal communication (February 1979).

Watson, Jane Werner; Switzer, Robert E.; and Hirschberg, J. Cotter. *Sometimes I'm Jealous.* Golden Press, New York (1972).

White, Robert W. Motivation reconsidered: the concept of competence. *Psychological Review* 66, (1959), 297–333.

Whiting, B., and Whiting, John W. M. *Children of Six Cultures.* Harvard University Press, Cambridge, Mass. (1975).

Yeats, William Butler. A prayer for my daughter (1921), in *Selected Poems and Two Plays of William Butler Yeats* (M. L. Rosenthal, ed.). Collier Books, New York (1962).

Index